America by Heart

ALSO BY SARAH PALIN

Going Rogue: An American Life

America by Heart

Reflections on Family, Faith, and Flag

Sarah Palin

HARPER LUXE

An Imprint of HarperCollins*Publishers*

HarperCollins books may be purchased for educational, business, or sales promotional use. For information please write: Special Markets Department, HarperCollins Publishers, 10 East 53rd Street, New York, NY 10022.

An extension of this copyright page appears on page 301.

FIRST HARPERLUXE EDITION

HarperLuxe™ is a trademark of HarperCollins Publishers

Library of Congress Cataloging-in-Publication Data is available upon request.

ISBN: 978-0-06-202640-8

10 11 12 13 14   ID/RRD   10 9 8 7 6 5 4 3 2 1

For Trig.
I'm glad you're here.

"If there must be trouble, let it be in my day, that my child may have peace."

—THOMAS PAINE, FOUNDING FATHER

CONTENTS

Introduction

AN AMERICAN AWAKENING

"Do you love your freedom?!"

The words rush out of me. It's a rhetorical question, of course. No one could look at this crowd of rowdy patriots waving American flags and chanting, "USA! USA!" and not know the answer. What's most amazing is that it's April 14, the day before Tax Day. We're in Boston, the home of the original American tax revolt. *And everyone is in such a good mood.* The crowd roars in the affirmative in answer to my question. And I look out on a sea of my fellow Americans:

grandmas, college students, moms, dads, kids, veterans, people in business suits—even an aging hippie or two.

"If you love your freedom, thank a vet." I ask all the men and women who have served or are serving our country in uniform to raise their hands. They wave, and the crowd explodes. "God bless you guys! We thank you. You're the reason we can be here today. We salute you!"

The mainstream media has been working overtime to portray these Americans as angry and bigoted. But I look out and see happy faces—faces of all ages, genders, and hues. The Stars and Stripes is everywhere, rippling in the spring breeze from outstretched arms and attached to wheelchairs and strollers. Dozens of yellow "Don't Tread on Me" flags glow in the morning sun.

But it's the hand-painted, homemade signs that say it all. They're everywhere. I see a young girl holding one that says, "STOP Spending Money I Haven't Earned Yet!" I see a young man holding a placard that says simply, "I'm Privileged to Be an American." One guy's sign jokes, "I Can See November from My House!" And an older lady holds up a copy of the Constitution with the message "When All Else Fails, Read the Instructions."

And my personal favorite, held by a mom with a stroller: "My Kid Is Not Your ATM."

What honest, heartfelt sentiments, I think. These people aren't an angry mob—they're Americans. Why do some feel the need to demonize them?

And then I see them, on the fringes of the crowd: the professionally printed signs held aloft by a few counter-protestors. What a difference. Unlike the humor, color, and variety of the hand-painted signs, the printed signs are all the same (with the exception of one guy, who, in an attempt at humor—or at least distraction—is holding up a life-size photo of Levi Johnston's center-fold). Written on those signs are the gripes of Washington special interest groups. The signs are held up by their hired stooges. And suddenly it comes to me: This is the central political struggle facing America today, being played out right here. With the exception of a few crackpots, the professionally printed signs all want something more from government—more for their union bosses, more for their special interest group, more for this government program or that.

In short, the people holding the uniformly printed signs have their hands out; Washington is spending away our kids' future and they still want more. But the people holding the homemade signs are the ones paying the bills. If the mainstream media wasn't busy insinuating that they're all racists and haters, it would have to acknowledge this fact. So the media keeps the coverage based on these patriots' motives. But what these good, honest Americans are asking for isn't ugly and dangerous. It's right there, on their signs and their flags and their faces, young and old and black and white: They want their country back.

I mention to the crowd that, this year, the Tax Day that matters isn't April 15, but April 9. That's the day the average American worker finally earns enough to pay his or her federal and state taxes, which means that the average American spends the first ninety-nine days of the year working for the government. The crowd's roar of response tells me that these Americans are feeling overtaxed by Washington. But I can tell that it isn't just high taxes that have brought these Americans here. Something bigger is going on, something much bigger.

My family and I have spent a lot of the past year traveling the country. I've visited dozens of cities in more than half of the fifty states on a tour for my first book, *Going Rogue*, helping out candidates running for office, and promoting pro-American causes. My visit to Boston was the next-to-last stop of the Tea Party Express in a forty-four-city, three-week tour. I was there when the tour began, in the desert sands of Searchlight,

Nevada, when more than ten thousand citizens turned out to take back their government. And I was there in Boston for one last rally before the tour ended on Tax Day in (where else, when the issue is "taking back our government"?) Washington, D.C.

Along the way, I've talked to literally thousands of Americans from all across the country. I've met with folks in their living rooms, at their businesses, and at boisterous, country-music-jammin' rallies. What's more, hundreds of people have sent me books, magazine articles, snippets of speeches, and their own comments with different takes on America.

What I've learned from all this traveling and meeting and talking and reading is this: the spark of patriotic indignation that inspired the Americans who fought for our freedom and independence has been ignited once again! Americans are reawakening to the ideas, the principles, the habits of the heart, and disciplines of the mind that made America great. This isn't a political awakening. It's an *American* awakening. It's coming from real people—not politicos or inside-the-Beltway types. These are the Americans who grow our food, teach our children, run our small businesses, help out those less fortunate, and fight our wars. They've seen what is happening in America, so they've decided to get involved. They feel like they're losing something good and fundamental about their country, so they've decided to take it back, because they love this country and are proud to be Americans!

One of my first clues to how real and how consequential this awakening is came from my own, independent-minded family. My uncle Ron and aunt Kate are businesspeople in Washington State. They're not particularly political; they'd never been intimately involved with any party or movement. So when I found out they had attended Tea Party meetings, in the very, very early stages of this "people's movement," I knew it was time to ask: Who are these participants? And I realized that the Tea Partiers *are* my uncle Ron and aunt Kate: normal Americans who haven't necessarily been involved in national politics before but are turned on to this movement because they love America and they don't like what they see happening to her. They're so concerned about the path we're on that they've decided to get involved. And believe me; they may not have done this two years ago. But they're doing it today.

Just like at the rally in Boston, taxing and spending are the most frequent subjects of Tea Partiers' signs and speeches. But Americans are coming to understand that the irresponsible fiscal path we're on is just a symptom of a more serious disease. People approach me all the time to tell me they're worried that we're losing what's best about our country. President Obama and the current Washington crowd have promised us a "fundamental transformation of America." The Left seems to think that there's something wrong with America—not something wrong with our policies or our government, but something wrong with our country and what we value. So they're hell-bent on changing it. They don't seem to share the timeless values that so many of us hold dear: our belief in our God-given freedom, our faith in free markets, and our certainty that the truths of our American founding are the way to a more perfect union.

A friend sent me a perfect illustration of this mindset. It was a copy of the U.S. Constitution that was purchased with this *warning label* printed on the back: "This book is a product of its time and does not reflect the same values as it would if it were written today. Parents might wish to discuss with their children how views on race, gender, sexuality, ethnicity, and interpersonal relations have changed since this book was written before allowing them to read this classic work."

That's right: a warning label attached to the Constitution of the United States! It's outrageous, but in a sense it's a perfect reflection of the thinking of those who believe America needs a "fundamental transformation." They believe that the ideas of limited government and personal liberty that are contained in documents like the Constitution are dangerous and outdated. They honestly believe that our founding ideas and documents are obstacles to their vision of America. The Constitution doesn't reflect their values because it is a document that fundamentally constrains government. So they work to get around those constraints. They put warning labels on those constraints.

But here is what you'll learn if you'll take the time to go out and see this big, beautiful country: Americans still "cling" (to use a word that's been used before) to our founding values. We don't want a fundamental transformation. America has problems—real ones. People are hurting and out of work. Families are struggling to pay their bills and save for the future. But what's wrong with America isn't that we're America. Our country doesn't need to change to get us back on track. It's our leadership and its political focus that need to change.

It's not necessary to participate in a multistate listening tour to feel the economic anxiety in the country. It should be obvious what's motivating people like my uncle Ron and aunt Kate to come out and speak their minds: but it isn't just fear about losing jobs and homes; it's much more than that.

We're worried about our families, and whether as a country we are honoring the role and responsibility of mothers and fathers. We're worried that we're not protecting the innocence and safety of children. And we're worried that their future opportunities are being thwarted by shortsighted political decisions being made today.

We're concerned about seeing that our laws are applied, equally and fairly, to everyone.

We're worried that government and big business are in bed together; that the little guy no longer has a fair shot in America.

We're concerned that in our quest to have freedom *of* religion, we are becoming a country of freedom *from* religion.

And we're worried that our leaders don't believe what we believe: that America is an exceptional nation, the shining city on a hill that Ronald Reagan believed it is. Our current leaders like to focus on America's faults and apologize for her shortcomings—both real and perceived—to dictators and would-be dictators abroad. We know our country isn't perfect, but we also know that Abraham Lincoln was right when he called it "the last best hope of earth." We want leaders who share this fundamental belief. We deserve such leaders.

These are the concerns of Tea Party Americans and anyone else who understands how dangerous it is to erode our Constitution's foundational principles.

I've noticed something since I've been out on the road. I give a lot of speeches and talk about a lot of things. I talk about how Washington spending is sticking our kids and grandkids with the tab for politicians' irresponsibility. I talk about our need for energy independence. And okay, I'll admit it: I talk a lot about Todd and my wonderful kids and my beautiful grandbaby. But the thing that gets the most enthusiastic response— the words that get people on their feet and cheering —is when I talk about America's founding ideas and documents. Just one mention of the Constitution and audiences go wild with appreciation for our Charter of Liberty.

I think I've figured out the reason why. I have a kind of internal compass that keeps me sane and grounded when the media attack dogs bark and the days on the road get long. No surprise, I keep my internal compass pointed due north, to where my roots are. My family and my faith are my greatest sources of support. They are my true north.

I've thought and read a lot more about what it means to be an American since I was given the honor of being nominated to help lead her in 2008. What I've come to realize is that, as a country, our true north is the values and principles on which we were founded— those values that are under attack today. When times are uncertain—when we're worried about the direction our country is headed in, as we are today—we can always turn to these fundamental principles. Truth be told, they're old ideas, not just the notion that our government should be limited, but also that all men and women are equal before the law; that life is sacred; and that God is the source of our rights, not government. The wonder of America is that these old ideas created a nation that is always new, always innovating and moving forward. That is the miracle of America.

And the source of this miracle can be found in those "dangerous" documents—our "Charters of Liberty"—the Declaration of Independence, the Constitution, and the Bill of Rights. Most of us studied these documents in school, but I've noticed that many Americans are turning to them for inspiration and guidance today. At Tea Party events, people pass out copies of the Constitution like candy. And when I've spoken to other groups and attended their events, I've noticed that more and more have made defending our founding principles a main part of their mission. Americans who believe in the sanctity of life and advocate for the unborn, for example, no longer simply call themselves "pro-life." Now they're "pro-life and pro-Constitution." Folks who care about the environment aren't just "pro-conservation" anymore. Now they're "pro-conservation and pro-Constitution." And those Americans clinging to their guns? They're not just "pro–Second Amendment." They're "pro" the whole darn thing.

I'm not the first American to notice this, of course. A friend recently sent me a speech given by one of our most overlooked presidents, Calvin Coolidge. Silent Cal had it nailed way back in 1926. Here's what he said on the 150th anniversary of the signing of the Declaration of Independence:

> Amid all the clash of conflicting interests, amid all the welter of partisan politics, every American can turn for solace and consolation to the Declaration of Independence and the Constitution of the United States with the assurance and confidence that those two great charters of freedom and justice remain firm and unshaken. Whatever perils appear, whatever dangers threaten, the Nation remains secure in the knowledge that the ultimate application of the law of the land will provide an adequate defense and protection.

Americans are awakening again to the wisdom of President Coolidge and that sweet old lady at the Boston Tea Party rally holding up a copy of the Constitution:

"When All Else Fails, Read the Instructions."

When we take the time to actually read them, the instructions for America are pretty straightforward. They are the truths of our founding and more. They are the principles that have made our country great—keeping our government limited, our markets free, and our families strong. But the thing is, these principles, like all fundamental human truths, are not self-reinforcing. They have to be remembered, cherished, and taught to new generations of Americans.

Moms know better than most that we are all born unformed and fallen. Any parent of a two-year-old knows her child's potential for both good and bad. And every parent of a high school graduate or a young soldier, sailor, airman, or Marine knows the sense of pride and accomplishment that comes with raising a good and decent child. Molding the crooked timber of humanity requires the grace of God, the patience of caring parents, and the dedication of good teachers. Creating a great nation from the diverse peoples who make America requires a strong sense of who we are and what we believe in. We have to know this, remember it, and teach it.

We have to know what makes America exceptional today more than ever because it is under assault today more than ever.

When I was preparing for my debate with then-vice-presidential candidate Joe Biden during the 2008 campaign I came across a quote from Ronald Reagan that perfectly expresses our need to preserve and protect American values. I quickly memorized it so I could use it for my closing statement, knowing that seventy million viewers would listen and learn from Reagan's wise words:

> Freedom is never more than one generation away from extinction. We didn't pass it to our children in the bloodstream. It must be fought for, protected, and handed on for them to do the same, or one day we will spend our sunset years telling our children and our children's children what it was once like in the United States when men were free.

I can't think of a sadder prospect for Todd and me than our spending our sunset years telling our grandson, Tripp, and our grandchildren yet to come about what it was like in America when we were strong and proud and free.

But maybe I *can* think of a sadder prospect: Tripp and our other grandchildren spending their whole lives working to pay off the irresponsible debt we have accumulated and are about to leave to them.

Neither of these futures is one I want for my grandchildren. Fortunately, I have been given a great gift, the gift of seeing this amazing country up close and personal, in a way that few Americans can. When I began writing this book, I thought carefully about the many wonderful folks I'd met over the past couple of years, and I reread the articles, books, and devotionals they'd shared with me. I also asked some of the people I love and trust to share with me the stories, the characters, and the words that form their view of America. I've been amazed at some of the things I've learned, comforted by much of it, and challenged in my views more than once.

And when I took these bits and pieces of Americana and blended them with my own experiences and views, I came up with this book. It's my view of America and what has made her great. It's the ideas our country was founded on. It's the strength of our families. It's the grit of our national character. It's our faith in God, how it has shaped our nation and continues to fortify us as a people.

President Reagan's call for us to fight for, protect, and pass on to future generations the sources and meaning of our freedom is both a political and a personal call; it is a challenge, both for our country and for us individually. I take this challenge seriously. Passing on peace, prosperity, and liberty to the next generation requires a strong military, a free market, and a healthy constitutional order. But none of that will be sufficient if our children are not taught to have a reverence for the ideas, ideals, and traditions that are central to the American experiment.

This is my America, from my heart, and by my heart. I give it now to my children and grandchildren, and to yours, so they will always know what it was like in America when people were free.

America by Heart

One

WE THE PEOPLE

When I was elected governor of Alaska in 2006, my friend Bruce, who'd helped out on the campaign, presented me with a black-and-white framed print of Jefferson Smith, the character played by Jimmy Stewart in the Frank Capra film *Mr. Smith Goes to Washington*. It hung on my wall in the governor's office in Juneau, and it hangs on my office wall in Wasilla today.

Call it corny, but *Mr. Smith Goes to Washington* is one of my favorite movies. It's a movie about hope. It's a movie about good triumphing over evil and idealism defeating cynicism. Most of all, it's a movie about the timeless truths of America handed down to us from our forefathers and foremothers.

In other words, it's a movie Hollywood would never make today.

In case you've forgotten, *Mr. Smith* is about an American Everyman, Jefferson Smith, who goes to Washington to fill the Senate seat of a corrupt senator who died in office. The political machine chooses Smith because he is an ordinary man, a nonpolitician, and they think they can control him. But he holds fast to his ideals—the ideals of the American founding—and eventually defeats the machine. The movie was made in 1939, but its message is timeless: there may be corruption in politics, but it can be overcome by decent men and women who honor America's founding principles, the way the American people do.

No doubt, most of today's Hollywood hotshots think movies like *Mr. Smith* are sappy and uncool, foolish sentimentalism about a country they seem to prefer to run down rather than build up. During the Iraq War, Hollywood produced a whole slew of movies that portrayed the United States (read: the Bush administration) as motivated by vengeance and oil, with the troops as mindless pawns. But almost all of them bombed at the box office, because most Americans don't share this view of our country or our troops. The same cultural gap exists with *Mr. Smith Goes to Washington*. Americans love this movie. More than seventy years later, we still watch it and judge Washington against it, because it is happily, unabashedly pro-American—not pro-government, certainly, but definitely pro-American. It celebrates the values that have come to us from our founding and that have made our country great.

The wonderful thing about *Mr. Smith Goes to Washington* is that it doesn't just cheerlead for America, or engage in a theoretical discussion of our founding documents, the Declaration of Independence and the Constitution. It puts these documents and their ideas into a human context. It shows us all the love, charity, and humanity that they embody when they are honored and adhered to.

I shared a love of this movie with my maternal grandfather, C. J. Sheeran. One of our favorite scenes comes in the middle of Senator Smith's famous filibuster. It is a scene that has not only inspired a love of democratic ideals in generations of Americans but also provided them a basic education in the nature of congressional debate. Smith is trying to get a loan from the federal government to build a boys' camp on some land where the corrupt political machine in his state, headed by a Mr. James Taylor, is eyeing to build a dam. Taylor has bought off most of Senator Smith's colleagues, but Smith refuses to back down. In the scene, Jimmy Stewart reads verbatim the opening words of the Declaration of Independence on the floor of the Senate. Then he challenges his colleagues to honor what these words mean in human terms, because, as he says, "you're not gonna have a country that can make these kind of rules work if you haven't got men that have learned to tell human rights from a punch in the nose."

Senator Smith doesn't want to build a camp so that boys can discover their inner selves or learn to worship Mother Earth. He wants to build a boys camp to help produce young men willing and capable of living together in freedom in a country in which they are endowed by their Creator with certain inalienable rights:

And it seemed like a pretty good idea, getting boys from all over the country, boys of all nationalities and ways of living—getting them together. Let them find out what makes different people tick the way they do. Because I wouldn't give you two cents for all your fancy rules if, behind them, they didn't have a little bit of plain, ordinary, everyday kindness and a little lookin' out for the other fella, too.

That's pretty important, all that. It's just the

blood and bone and sinew of this democracy that some great men handed down to the human race, that's all!

Jefferson Smith loves the words of the Declaration of Independence, not because he's mindlessly pro-American, but because, as he says, "behind them, they . . . have a little bit of plain, ordinary, everyday kindness and a little lookin' out for the other fella, too." He understands that those words are a gift, not just to Americans, but to all humanity. But that gift is being corrupted by special interests and forgotten by Washington.

That's what I think so many of the people who make the big laws, run the big corporations, write for the big newspapers, and make the big movies today have forgotten. Americans love this country because it means something, and it has since the beginning. That meaning, many of us feel, is being lost today.

Americans love *Mr. Smith Goes to Washington* because it's about an ordinary man who stands up to power and says, *We're taking our country back.*

It seems like ancient history now, but I remember it vividly. I was a young mother—Track had just been born—and I was watching a revolution on television.

It was 1989 when it began. First in Poland, then in Czechoslovakia, Hungary, East Germany, and Romania—the dominoes of dictatorship fell. And then, soon after the decade turned, the Soviet Union—the dictatorship that was responsible for all the other fallen dictatorships—met its fate. I watched in August 1991 as Boris Yeltsin stood on a tank outside the Kremlin and faced down a coup by Communist hard-liners. By New Year's Day 1992, the Soviet Empire was no more.

It was a dizzying moment to be free. For my entire life, Americans had been told by the propaganda mouthpieces of the Communist regimes—not to mention plenty of others in the free world—that Soviet communism was the way of the future. We had been told it was a more just and democratic form of government because it guaranteed the equality of all. We had been told that it was Americans, not the Russians or the Poles or the Chinese, who were living in an authoritarian society. After all, the Soviet constitution promised its citizens dozens of rights, including the right to work, the right to leisure, the right to health care and housing, and some rights that sound very familiar to Americans, such as freedom of speech, press, and religion.

None of these rights meant anything in the Soviet Union, of course. They were words on paper and nothing more. The reason, I think, is important for Americans to understand. It speaks as much to the wonderful uniqueness of our Constitution as it does to the hollowness of the Soviet document.

In 1987, just a few years before the Soviet Empire began to fall, America celebrated the two-hundredth anniversary of our Constitution. That year, in his State of the Union Address, President Reagan talked with his usual courage and clarity about the special magic of the American Constitution:

I've read the constitutions of a number of countries, including the Soviet Union's. Now, some people are surprised to hear that they have a constitution, and it even supposedly grants a number of freedoms to its people. Many countries have written into their constitution provisions for freedom of speech and freedom of assembly. Well, if this is true, why is the Constitution of the United States so exceptional?

Well, the difference is so small that it almost escapes you, but it's so great it tells you the whole story in just three words: *We the people.* In those other constitutions, the Government tells the people of those countries what they're allowed to do. In our Constitution, we the people tell the

Government what it can do, and it can do only those things listed in that document and no others. Virtually every other revolution in history has just exchanged one set of rulers for another set of rulers. Our revolution is the first to say the people are the masters and government is their servant.

History has borne out the truth of President Reagan's words. In the USSR, the government used its constitution to tell the people what they could do—to grant them so-called rights. It said the Soviet people had a "right" to just about everything. But of course, if a government can grant you a right, it can also take that right away. And that's what the dictators of the Soviet Empire did: they promised their people the moon, but in the end it was the government, not the people, that had the power. It could choose to give its people rights or not, and it chose not to, so the people finally rose up.

It's different here, and the reason is our Constitution. I remember memorizing the preamble to the Constitution when I was a little girl in Alaska, watching *Schoolhouse Rock* at a friend's house. What I was just beginning to learn about our Constitution is that it doesn't *give* us rights—it describes a government that protects our God-given rights. It puts us in charge. As Newt Gingrich likes to note, our Constitution doesn't begin "We the government of the United States . . ." or "We the federal bureaucrats of the United States . . ." or "We the special interests camped out on Capitol Hill of the United States . . ." It begins like this:

> We the People of the United States, in Order to form a more perfect Union, establish Justice, insure domestic Tranquility, provide for the common defense, promote the general Welfare, and secure the Blessings of Liberty to ourselves and our Posterity, do ordain and establish this Constitution for the United States of America.

As usual, the Gipper absolutely hit the nail on the head. The difference, with our Constitution, is those three little words: *We the people.*

What has struck me most in traveling around the country in the past two years is the tremendous, unshakable love Americans have for their country, even when times are tough, and even when we are most definitely out of love with Washington, D.C.

It says something interesting about Americans that this love of country so often takes the form of love of our Founders and our founding documents. Everyone claims to love the Founders, of course. But so many of our so-called academic and cultural elite talk out of both sides of their mouths when it comes to the founding. They pay lip service to revered American figures such as George Washington and Thomas Jefferson at the same time that they bad-mouth the principles they stood for. They think Americans such as James Madison and Alexander Hamilton are museum pieces, interesting historical figures with no relevance to our lives today.

You're probably familiar with their take on America's founding. They think the Declaration of Independence and the Constitution are just documents written by old white men to benefit other old white men. To really have a just and equal society, they argue, we have to change these documents, update them for the times, and make them no longer mean what the Americans who wrote them intended them to mean. Either that, or we have to ignore them altogether.

I hear from and meet Americans every day who have a very different view. They see America as having flaws, to be sure. But they understand that these flaws are not in the nature of our country but in the nature of humanity. No government can—or should try to—change our fundamental human nature. Deliverance is for the next life. You don't have to look any further than the killing fields of Cambodia, the gulags of Soviet

Russia, or the mass starvation of Communist China to see what happens when government tries to remake men and women.

The wonderful thing about the system we inherited from the Founders is that it doesn't try to change our humanity; rather, it respects it and honors it. This is the approach our Founders took from the very beginning, when they announced the birth of America with, next to the Bible, the most consequential words for human freedom ever written:

We hold these truths to be self-evident, that all men are created equal, that they are endowed by their Creator with certain unalienable Rights, that among these are Life, Liberty and the pursuit of Happiness.—That to secure these rights, Governments are instituted among Men, deriving their just powers from the consent of the governed,— That whenever any Form of Government becomes destructive of these ends, it is the Right of the People to alter or to abolish it, and to institute new Government, laying its foundation on such principles and organizing its powers in such form, as to them shall seem most likely to effect their Safety and Happiness. Prudence, indeed, will dictate that Governments long established should not be changed for light and transient causes; and accordingly all experience hath shewn that mankind are more disposed to suffer, while evils are sufferable, than to right themselves by abolishing the forms to which they are accustomed. But when a long train of abuses and usurpations, pursuing invariably the same Object evinces a design to reduce them under absolute Despotism, it is their right, it is their duty, to throw off such Government, and to provide new Guards for their future security.

I still get chills when I read these words. They express a beautiful idea—that we are all equally precious in the eyes of our Creator—that gave birth to a beautiful country.

"We hold these truths to be self-evident, that all men are created equal, that they are endowed by their Creator with certain unalienable Rights . . ."

It is to keep faith with these words that our Constitution begins "We the people." In America, the people are sovereign, not just as a group, but individually. We are endowed by our Creator with this sovereignty. That means no person, no king and no government, can rule us without our consent. We all have a right to life, liberty, and the pursuit of happiness that wasn't given to us by government; it was given to us by God. Therefore, it can't rightly be taken away by government.

To me, the Declaration of Independence is an expression of our ideals as a nation—the ideals of liberty and equality—and the Constitution is how we make those ideals a reality. I found a great metaphor Abraham Lincoln used to describe the relationship between the Declaration of Independence and the Constitution in Matthew Spalding's wonderful book *We Still Hold These Truths.*

To illustrate how the Declaration and the Constitution work together, Lincoln cited Proverbs 25:11: "A word fitly spoken is like apples of gold in a setting of silver." For Lincoln, the principles of the Declaration—that we are granted by our Creator with inalienable rights—are the apples of gold. "The *Union,* and the *Constitution,*" Lincoln wrote, "are the *picture of silver,* subsequently framed around it. The *picture* was made *for* the apple—*not* the apple for the picture."

For me, this is the essence of freedom: to be a child of God whose God-given rights and responsibilities are respected by her government under the Constitution. What makes all of us Americans isn't our ancestry or our skin color but our belief in this freedom. This isn't the kind of freedom that says, "Whatever feels good, just do it." It's the kind of freedom that says, "Don't tread on me." It's the kind of freedom that shouts that men and women aren't just as free as their government or their king will allow them to be. Freedom is our birthright. We are free as a consequence of being made in the image of God—even if you don't believe in God. Not only that, but we are equally free; no person or group of persons is less free than any other.

Too many voices in America today sound the wrong-headed belief that these truths are no longer so self-evident. Some of these voices come from Washington, but many more come from our universities, our high school textbooks, even our churches. These skeptics think we have outgrown our founding principles, that even the wisest men and women in 1776 and 1787 couldn't possibly have been wise enough to create an effective government for America in the twenty-first century.

Some find the words of the Founders too limiting for their bloated vision of government. After all, government that is true to the ideals of our Charters of Liberty is government that is limited. If government exists to protect our God-given rights—and not to bail out big banks, buy car companies, take over our health care, and tell us which lightbulbs we can use—then that government does a few things, does them well, and gets out of the way in order to allow its citizens to realize their potential.

Remember the 2001 interview about the Constitution by then–Illinois state senator Barack Obama that surfaced during the 2008 campaign? In it, Senator Obama complained as he captured perfectly the constraints on government created by the Constitution. Speaking about the Supreme Court in the 1950s and '60s during the civil rights movement, Obama expressed regret that the High Court

> never ventured into the issues of redistribution of wealth, and of more basic issues of political and economic justice in society. To that extent, as radical as I think people try to characterize the Warren Court, it wasn't that radical. *It didn't break free from the essential constraints that were placed by the Founding Fathers in the Constitution, at least as it's been interpreted, and the Warren Court interpreted it the same way, that generally the Constitution is a charter of negative liberties. Says what the states can't do to you. Says what the federal government can't do to you,* but it doesn't say what the federal government or the state government must do on your behalf. (emphasis mine)

Our future president called the civil rights movement's focus on the courts—and the courts' subsequent failure to break free of the constraints imposed by the

Constitution—a "tragedy." But a lot of us call it basic fairness and adherence to our founding principles. We believe it's a good thing that we came so far in achieving racial justice while keeping faith with our Constitution.

Some like to dismiss all this talk about staying true to our founding documents as the ideological rants of people who are obsessed with constitutional theory. But whether we remain true to our Constitution or not has practical, real-world consequences for all of us.

The Supreme Court, along with the rest of the federal judiciary, has tremendous power over our lives today. Their rulings mean the difference between free political speech and censored political speech, property rights that are protected by government and property rights that are routinely violated by government, and the survival of innocent life and the state-sanctioned killing of innocent life. The reason this is the case is because so many of the people who appoint and approve our judges and justices erroneously believe the courts' duty isn't to interpret the law but to *make* the law. In cases where their agenda can't prevail among the people's representatives in Congress, they have turned to the courts to make policy. That means having judges and justices who are no longer guided by the Constitution and the law, but by their personal opinions. President Obama himself has said that, in the really difficult, consequential cases, justices shouldn't go with the law but with their hearts. "That last mile can only be determined on the basis of one's deepest values, one's core concerns, one's broader perspectives on how the world works, and the depth and breadth of one's empathy," the president said.

But if you look at the oath of office that every Supreme Court justice takes, you see that it commits them to a very different standard. They pledge not to pick winners and losers based on their hearts or their "empathy," but to impartially apply the Constitution and the law. Here is their oath:

> I, (name), do solemnly swear (or affirm) that I will administer justice without respect to persons, and do equal right to the poor and to the rich, and that I will faithfully and impartially discharge and perform all the duties incumbent upon me as Supreme Court Justice under the Constitution and laws of the United States. So help me God.

When you take the time to read the plain text of this oath, and then consider many of the criteria that President Obama and other progressives have spelled out for their judges and Supreme Court justices, there

other conclusion to come to other than that pro-
ssives want Supreme Court justices who will *violate*
eir oath of office.

Now, empathy is certainly a good and virtuous
thing. It's something we should practice ourselves, and
look for in our doctors, our teachers, and our neighbors. But should empathy be the guiding criterion for
our judges? After all, one person's empathy may be another person's antipathy. Our Constitution spells out a
separation of powers between Congress, the president,
and the judiciary for a very good reason: to protect our
freedom and our right to govern ourselves from one
person's idea of "empathy." When we give more power
to unelected judges, we take power away from "we the
people."

It's no accident that progressives view the Constitution
and the Declaration of Independence as obstacles to be
mowed down or maneuvered around to create bigger
government. After all, their name itself, progressives,
implies that there is something defective or at least in-
adequate about America. Progressives exist, their name
implies, to "correct" America and to "correct" all the
rest of us in the process.

The epitome of progressive thinking was Barack
Obama's promise, just before the 2008 election, that

"we are five days away from fundamentally transforming the United States of America." I guess you could say he warned us! But the problem is that Americans don't want a fundamental transformation of their country. Americans are awakening to the fact that, of course our country has changed a great deal since it was born, but our Founders hit on some timeless truths that will never change and should never change. More and more of us view our founding truths as a bulwark, not just against bigger government, but against losing that fundamental sense of decency that Senator Smith fought for. If we forget these truths—or reject that they are timeless—we lose something fundamental about ourselves. No, "transformation" won't save America; "restoration" of our honor, dignity, and freedoms will save America.

Every generation thinks it is having its arguments for the first time. In fact, our old friend Calvin Coolidge—is it just a coincidence that one of the presidents who most appreciated our founding principles is one of the least celebrated by the academic elite?—made this point over 80 years ago. In the same speech I cited earlier, the one celebrating the 150th anniversary of the signing of the Declaration of Independence (which is full of interesting nuggets; I highly recommend it), President Coolidge delivered a devastating rebuke to those who thought the principles of our founding were no longer relevant way back in 1926:

> It is often asserted that the world has made a great deal of progress since 1776, that we have had new thoughts and new experiences which have given us great advance over the people of that day, and that we may therefore very well discard their conclusions for something more modern. But that reasoning can not be applied to this great charter [the Declaration of Independence]. If all men are created equal, that is final. If they are endowed with inalienable rights, that is final. If governments derive their just powers from the consent of the governed, that is final. No advance, no progress can be made beyond these propositions. If anyone wishes to deny their truth or their soundness, the only direction in which he can proceed historically is not forward, but backward toward the time when there was no equality, no rights of the individual, no rule of the people. Those who wish to proceed in that direction can not lay claim to progress. They are reactionary. Their ideas are not more modern, but more ancient, than those of the Revolutionary fathers.

It's worth asking: Who are the real "progressives" in America today? As President Coolidge said, to deny the principles of our founding isn't to go forward (to "progress") but to go "backward toward the time when there was no equality, no rights of the individual, no rule of the people." Those who run down American values and think our founding principles are somehow intolerant or theocratic have it exactly backward. The words of the Declaration of Independence, brought to life in the words of the Constitution, are the most liberating, most human-rights-respecting words ever written. They assert the moral and political equality of all men and women, no matter who their parents are or how much money they have. What could be more "progressive" than that?

What's most amazing to me is that I think most Americans understand this. Most Americans don't just blindly love their country; they understand the unique gift of freedom it represents and they strive to live up to it. The men and women of our military make sacrifices to defend this freedom every day. But ordinary Americans do so as well, by resisting trading their freedom for the promise of cradle-to-grave government security the way so many countries of Western Europe have. Americans don't just cling to their liberty like spoiled children. We understand that freedom isn't free. It's one of the many things about the American people our politicians underestimate.

Take the recent health care debate as an example. The folks pushing President Obama's government health care bill seemed to think that we could be bought. But when we say we believe that our rights are God-given it means something. Those words in the Declaration of Independence mean that our rights are sacred; government can't legitimately violate them or add to them. The proponents of government health care didn't seem to think that Americans understood this principle—or, if we understood it, we didn't really mean it. They seemed to think we could be bribed by pie-in-the-sky promises; that we were gullible enough to believe that government could manufacture a new "right" to health care and we wouldn't pay the price with our freedom, such as our freedom to keep what we earn, to choose our own doctor, and to buy—or not buy—health insurance.

They were wrong, and for proof you don't have to look any further than the shameful way in which Obamacare was written and passed. It was written in secret, behind closed doors, far from the promised C-SPAN cameras. And it wasn't long before we found out why: To win the support of nervous politicians, President Obama, House Speaker Nancy Pelosi, and Senate

Majority Leader Harry Reid had to resort to trading pork in the bill for votes, cutting sleazy deals behind closed doors like the infamous "Louisiana Purchase" (in which a Louisiana senator's vote for the bill was secured in exchange for $300 million in extras for that state) and the "Cornhusker Kickback" (in which a Nebraska senator's vote was secured in a similar fashion). Not only that, but to pass the bill, congressional Democrats had to resort to all kinds of legislative shenanigans to avoid an up-or-down vote. At one point, Speaker Pelosi told a national audience that we'd have to pass the bill to "find out what's in it." She even hatched a plan to pass the bill without the House ever actually voting on it! And why? Because the support in Congress wasn't there. And the support in Congress wasn't there because public support wasn't there. The American people have a principled wisdom that all the lawyers and academics and schooled-up "experts" in D.C. fail to appreciate. Washington may have managed to make it the law, but we still don't support Obamacare. It turns out we can't be so easily bought.

Still, the bill was passed and the damage has been done. In the end, this unsustainable bill jeopardizes the very thing it was supposed to fix: our health care system. Somewhere along the way we forgot that health care reform is about doctors and patients, not the IRS and politicians. Instead of helping doctors with tort reform, this bill has made primary care physicians think about getting out of medicine. It was supposed to make health care more affordable, but our premiums will continue to go up. It was supposed to help more people get coverage, but there will still be twenty-three million uninsured people by 2019.

Americans have been reminded many times that elections have consequences, and Obamacare was definitely one of them. But as my father would say, instead of retreating, Americans are reloading. We don't consider the health care vote a done deal, not by a long shot. Instead, it was a clarion call, a spur to action. We will not let America sink further into debt caused by government controlling another one sixth of our economy—and mandating its approved health care coverage—without a fight. We will not abandon the American dream to government dependency, fewer freedoms, and less opportunity.

If our current leadership in Washington had ventured outside the Beltway more, they would have known that Americans are serious about our freedom. And we have the common sense to know there's no free lunch. As usual, a sign I spotted at a health care reform rally (held up by a guy I'm pretty sure wasn't a constitutional law professor) said it best: "Governments Don't Give Rights. Governments Take Rights Away."

There, written in black acrylic paint on neon poster board, was as good a description of what it takes to defend our freedom as I have ever seen. The giant that is America has been awakened.

The worst thing you can say about a fellow American in politics today is that he is a racist. It just doesn't get any more damning than this accusation. That's why so many of us were horrified to hear news reports that people protesting the passage of the health care bill had shouted racial epithets at an African American congressman as he walked to the Capitol to cast his vote. It was a serious charge, made by supposedly serious men, and repeated endlessly in the mainstream media. At a critical moment in the debate, it overshadowed all the arguments that opponents of Obamacare had made— that the bill would put government in control of our health care, cost too much, and explode the deficit. The racism charge painted opponents of the law with the lowest form of hate, not the best interests of their country or their neighbor.

But was it true? Despite the fact that everyone walks around these days with a cell phone capable of capturing video, evidence to support the charge has never emerged. In the weeks and months after the alleged incident, conservative blogger Andrew Breitbart even offered huge cash rewards to anyone who could produce proof that the health care protestors had shouted racial slurs. No proof ever emerged.

But a lack of evidence hasn't stopped liberal activists and their allies in the media from repeatedly accusing patriotic Americans at Tea Party rallies and elsewhere of being racists. And let's not kid ourselves. The purpose of this charge isn't to clarify but to confuse. It's thrown out there to shut down debate by declaring one side of it (dissenters from the Obama agenda) unworthy of being taken seriously. After all, if we're motivated only by the fact that there is a "black man in the White House" and not by serious policy differences, what's the point in discussing those policy differences? This tactic is of a piece with the shameful tendency on the left not simply to declare their opponents wrong, but to declare them evil. Conservatives and liberals don't have honest policy disagreements, this strategy says; conservatives are just bad people.

But more Americans have opposed Obamacare than have supported it since the health care debate began. A majority of Americans opposed the bill when it was proposed, then passed. A majority oppose it today. Does that mean that a majority of Americans are bad people? And would that be the same majority of Americans who voted for Barack Obama for president?

The deep unrest in America today wasn't caused by

the color of the president's skin but the content of his policies. And more and more, it seems that the starting point for these policies is the liberal view that the Constitution is a flawed document. One of the main arguments that the Constitution is flawed and no longer relevant is directly related to the issue of race. It's an issue that all admirers of the Constitution and of our founding have to deal with squarely and honestly: the Constitution's initial compromise on the issue of slavery.

It sometimes seems like slavery is all that liberal academics and the mainstream media want to talk about when the topic is America's birth, but that doesn't mean we shouldn't acknowledge the contradiction that slavery represented to American principles. To do less is to denigrate the greatness of those principles. To love our country is to confront our history squarely and honestly. To love our fellow Americans is to admit that we have not always, as a nation, respected their God-given rights.

Confronting our history, of course, also means acknowledging how much progress we've made as a nation to overcome the legacies of slavery and segregation. It always amazes me how some on the left would rather focus on America's sins rather than on the steps we've taken to heal and redeem them. Laws like the

1964 Civil Rights Act and the Voting Rights Act, which followed one year later, are great human achievements. They made our country better, not just for some of its citizens, but for all of its citizens. Wouldn't it be more constructive to celebrate these great achievements instead of dwelling obsessively on the problems that made them necessary in the first place?

In our hearts, I believe Americans are a fundamentally just and tolerant people. I've been to big cities and little towns throughout the country. I've met thousands of Americans. I've disagreed with some, agreed with more, and cherished (almost!) all of them. There are exceptions, of course, but in my experience, Americans are too busy raising their families, building their businesses, and looking after their neighbors to spend a lot of time fixating on the color of someone's skin.

Still, I don't think it's an accident that the opponents of this new American awakening so often accuse Tea Partiers and others of being racist. For one thing, it's a guaranteed conversation stopper. Just saying the word *racist* instantly ends any legitimate debate. Just the accusation gives the accuser an excuse not to debate the issues at hand.

The second reason the charge of racism is leveled at patriotic Americans so often is that the people making the charge actually believe it. They think America—at least America as it currently exists—is a fundamentally unjust and unequal country. Barack Obama seems to believe this, too. Certainly his wife expressed this view when she said during the 2008 campaign that she had never felt proud of her country until her husband started winning elections. In retrospect, I guess this shouldn't surprise us, since both of them spent almost two decades in the pews of the Reverend Jeremiah Wright's church listening to his rants against America and white people. It also makes sense, then, that the man President Obama made his attorney general, Eric Holder, would call us a "nation of cowards" for failing to come to grips with what he described as the persistence of racism.

Many on the left also believe that the current call for a smaller federal government and a return to federalism—otherwise known as states' rights—is code for a return to white supremacy.

But is it racist to believe in the principles of the American founding? To revere the Declaration of Independence, the Constitution, and the Bill of Rights and to invoke the Tenth Amendment? To want leaders and national policies that respect the wisdom and humanity of these documents?

The answer is important, because it speaks to the kind of country we are, and the kind of country we were meant to be. Did our founding values produce the country of Reverend Jeremiah Wright's rants? A place where African Americans or any minority would be justified in saying, "God damn America," instead of "God Bless America"?

Or did our Founders enshrine a set of principles that gave birth to a just society, despite the obscenity of slavery? Did they, in fact, set the stage for the elimination of slavery? Does America really need, in the words of President Obama, a "fundamental transformation" in order to be a good and decent nation?

As we all know, many of our Founders were slaveholders. Even Thomas Jefferson, the author of the assertion that all men are "created equal" and that we are all "endowed by our Creator with certain unalienable rights," owned slaves and may have had a sexual relationship with one of them.

Perhaps the most powerful (and frequently cited) evidence pointed to by critics of the founding is the so-called three-fifths clause in the original Constitution. The Constitution that was produced in Philadelphia in 1787 contained a clause that, for the purposes of determining representation in Congress and taxation, counted each "free person" as one and "all other persons" (meaning slaves, although the Constitution never uses the word) as three fifths of a person. Native Americans were not counted at all.

Americans can well ask how, in light of these historical facts, the idealistic words of the Declaration are not
the words of hypocrites? How can the meaning of the
Constitution not be that African Americans were, and
were destined to be, considered less human than white
Americans in the United States? If you've attended an
elite college or even taken a high school history course,
you have probably heard the infamous three-fifths
clause denounced as evidence that the founding generation was morally blind, thus all of their works are
irredeemably tainted, just like that label on the Constitution warned.

So what is the truth of our founding? We all know
that the question of what to do about slavery and its
obvious grotesque violation of the ideals of the Declaration was a major issue at the Constitutional Convention. It almost ended the Founders' efforts to produce a
Constitution, and with it, a new republic.

Most of us have always thought that the Founders
were forced to compromise on the issue of slavery for
the sake of creating the Union and keeping it together.
Some wanted slavery to continue; some genuinely
wanted it abolished. In the end, the profound moral
challenge of slavery was put off for future generations
to resolve.

To a great extent this view of the founding is true.
But what I've learned is that the framers of the Con-

stitution did more than simply compromise. They did more than just kick the can down the road. They produced a document that one of the delegates at the Constitutional Convention, James Wilson, said succeeded in "laying the foundation for banishing slavery out of this country," even though he regretted that "the period is more distant than I could wish."

Just how the framers did this was explained brilliantly in an essay by the late constitutional scholar Robert Goldwin:

> The struggle that took place in the convention was between Southern delegates trying to strengthen the constitutional supports for slavery and Northern delegates trying to weaken them. That issue— the initial and subsequent political strength of slavery—was in contention on the question of representation in the House of Representatives . . . Slave-state delegates were in favor of including every slave, just as they would any other inhabitant. Madison's notes indicate that the delegates from South Carolina "insisted that blacks be included in the rule of representation, equally with whites."
>
> On the other side, delegates from the nonslave states were opposed to counting the slaves, because it would give the South more votes and because it

made a mockery of the principle of representation to count persons who had no influence whatsoever on the law-making process and who therefore were not "represented" in the legislature in any meaningful sense of the word. Counting the slaves for purposes of representation would also give the slave states an incentive to increase their slave population instead of decreasing it. *In short, considering the chief purpose of this clause in the Constitution, it is obvious that an antislavery delegate would not want to count the slave at all.* (emphasis mine)

To our great and lasting shame, slavery continued in the United States for almost a century following the adoption of the Constitution. Although the controversy never went away, in the end it took the bloodiest war in our nation's history to end the evil practice. Hundreds of thousands of Americans died, but slavery finally died with them. And in an important and overlooked way, our Founders began this painful process.

In other words, when it comes to America, there is a difference between hating the sin and hating the sinner. To acknowledge honestly the stain of past slavery and racism is not the same thing as saying that America is a fundamentally racist country.

Barack Obama himself acknowledged as much in

his widely hailed speech on race during the 2008 campaign. Here's an excerpt that can be appreciated:

"We the people, in order to form a more perfect union."

Two hundred and twenty-one years ago, in a hall that still stands across the street, a group of men gathered and, with these simple words, launched America's improbable experiment in democracy. Farmers and scholars; statesmen and patriots who had traveled across an ocean to escape tyranny and persecution finally made real their declaration of independence at a Philadelphia convention that lasted through the spring of 1787.

The document they produced was eventually signed but ultimately unfinished. It was stained by this nation's original sin of slavery, a question that divided the colonies and brought the convention to a stalemate until the founders chose to allow the slave trade to continue for at least twenty more years, and to leave any final resolution to future generations.

Of course, the answer to the slavery question was already embedded within our Constitution—a Constitution that had at its very core the ideal of equal citizenship under the law; a Constitution that promised its people liberty, and justice, and a union that could be and should be perfected over time.

My only wish is that President Obama would follow through on this hopeful view of America. To want a better and brighter future for our country does not mean a rejection of our founding or a "fundamental transformation" of who we are. Instead it means following, in part, the wisdom of the most powerful American voice for civil rights of the twentieth century, the Reverend Dr. Martin Luther King, Jr. Famously, Dr. King called not for a rejection of America's founding principles, but for America to "rise up and live out the true meaning of its creed."

My first memory of hearing his words is sitting at my desk at Iditarod Elementary School. We had been studying the civil rights movement and were watching a grainy eight-millimeter film of Dr. King's speech projected onto a screen over the blackboard.

The events we watched were far away, both in time and space. The Washington Monument, for us, may as well have been the Eiffel Tower. I don't think any of us had ever been to our nation's capital, over four thousand miles from Alaska, but we knew something momentous had happened there a decade before, and that we were somehow a part of it. Dr. King's words made it so.

It wasn't our accomplishment; we knew that. The civil rights movement was the work of heroes we would never know except in history books. Still, Martin Luther King, Jr.'s, words made us feel like patriots that day.

> I have a dream that my four little children will one day live in a nation where they will not be judged by the color of their skin but by the content of their character.

King was speaking about the content of *our* character, and the meaning of *our* creed. We weren't there yet, but the fact that his dream was coming closer to reality made us so proud to be Americans. It made us want that dream for ourselves.

It's a shame that not everyone wants to quote Dr. King these days. What made Martin Luther King, Jr., a great and effective leader is that he appealed to our better angels. Unlike other so-called civil rights leaders who claim to be his heirs and to walk in his footsteps, he didn't doubt that America had it in her to be great. He just made us understand that to be great, we first had to be good. This man of God believed those words in the Declaration of Independence. He believed that our Creator had given us all the rights to life, liberty, and the pursuit of happiness. He knew that realizing his dream was the fulfillment of America's exceptional destiny. That's a belief, it seems to me, that shouldn't depend on whether someone is liberal or conservative or Republican or Democrat. It's an *American* belief.

It's a belief Senator Jefferson Smith would have agreed with.

TWO

WHY THEY SERVE

On September 11, 2007, my firstborn, my son Track, enlisted in the army. Exactly one year later, he and 3,500 fellow members of the First Stryker Brigade Combat Team, Twenty-fifth Infantry, deployed to Iraq from Fort Wainwright, Alaska.

Thirteen days earlier I had been chosen by John McCain as his vice-presidential running mate. I was both governor of Alaska and a vice-presidential candidate. That meant I had to convince the campaign honchos to let me fly home to see Track be deployed.

I had to travel with a security detail. I had to give a speech. The press wrote down my every move. Still, on that day, all the pomp and circumstance didn't matter. That day I was just one of thousands of proud but wary American women: I was the mom of a young soldier being sent overseas to defend our country.

That date, September 11, has so many connotations of sacrifice and service for Americans. So it made complete sense to me that it kept turning up in the course of Track's service. On September 11, 2008, the brigrade's deployment to Iraq landed the soldiers in the Diyala Province, northeast of Baghdad, fighting insurgents and helping to rebuild that war-torn country. Then, on September 11, 2009, he was scheduled to return home. Like all military families, his sisters, his baby brother, Todd, and I were overjoyed that Track was coming home safe. But at the last second, the family of one of the other members of the Stryker Brigade had a medical scare. Track's fellow soldier had to get home fast, and there were no extra seats on the transport. So Track, God bless him, gave up his seat. He had to stay an additional month in the heat and sand and danger of Iraq for another available flight home. At first, he didn't want to tell us about the reason for his delay. He still doesn't like to talk about it, much less have his mom crow about it in print. But when I finally heard the story of what he did for his fellow soldier, I think I was prouder of my son than I had ever been before.

When I think of Track and the young women and men he serves with, I am filled with a genuine sense of awe. What motivates these young people, most of whom have never known the absence of freedom, to risk their lives to defend it in a foreign land? Track and virtually all his fellow soldiers grew up knowing the freedom and security that comes with being an American. Most weren't rich, but they were certainly privileged to have homes, an education, and opportunities in life. I look at these kids and I think, *They could be off partying on spring break or working their way up a high-powered career ladder. What motivates them to put that all aside for a military enlistment?*

For Track, the reason he serves starts with his family. He has little sisters, a special baby brother, and a nephew. He wants a world that is safe and welcoming for them. I suspect the same is true for most American servicemen and -women. In my experience, Americans are patriotic but not necessarily ideological. We find inspiration and motivation close to home, in our families, our communities, and our faith. Generally, we're happy to live our lives and pursue our dreams and leave others to live and pursue theirs.

And if we were an ordinary country—just one country among many others—that would be enough. All countries have the right to defend themselves, and they exercise that right whenever necessary. But America isn't just another country, it's an exceptional country. We are the only country in the history of the world that was founded not on a particular territory or culture or people, but on an idea. That idea is that all human beings have a God-given right to be free. So when our young men and women sacrifice to serve in the military, they are doing much more than defending a piece of land. They are defending the idea of America itself.

It's this belief—that they are engaged in what my friend and former running mate John McCain calls "a cause bigger than themselves"—that motivates the American military.

In his book *The American Patriot's Almanac*, William Bennett—a pretty great patriot himself—singles out "Twelve Great Reasons to Love a Great Country." Bill's reason number seven makes my point:

> The U.S. military is the greatest defender of freedom in the world. Twice in the twentieth century, the United States led the way in saving the world from tyranny—first from the Axis Powers, then from Soviet totalitarianism. Throughout history, other superpowers have used armies to conquer

territory and build empires by force. America, with its unrivaled military, has chosen a different course. The United States has liberated more people from tyranny than any other nation in history.

This doesn't mean that Americans are eager for war—far from it. Believe me, nobody is more demanding when it comes to good reasons for going to war than our military moms. If you're going to send their sons and daughters into harm's way, you'd better have a darn good reason. I think most Americans share this belief. Which is why, contrary to the ugly accusations of the antiwar crowd, America doesn't go to war for big business or for oil or for the sake of imperial conquest.

The reason, inevitably, is freedom. Our attachment to liberty is part of our culture, a value we learn early in life and pass on to our kids and grandkids. The great French student of America, Alexis de Tocqueville, called liberty and freedom "habits of the heart." In other words, they're not values we come to through studying some great text or theory. It's a gut-level love we have; a stubborn attachment to a way of life that we're not about to give up. And it's our military that we turn to when this value is threatened.

There's a famous story about a conversation between a historian and a Revolutionary War veteran that I think captures very well what motivates our young men and women to fight to defend freedom.

It's 1843 and the young historian is interviewing a ninety-one-year-old veteran of the Battle of Lexington and Concord named Captain Levi Preston.

"Captain Preston," the historian asks, "what made you go to the Concord Fight? Were you oppressed by the Stamp Act?"

"I never saw any stamps," the old veteran growled, "and I always understood that none were ever sold."

"Well, what about the tea tax?"

"Tea tax? I never drank a drop of the stuff. The boys threw it all overboard."

"But I suppose you had been reading Harrington, Sidney, and Locke about the eternal principle of liberty?"

"I never heard of those men," Captain Preston answered gruffly. "The only books we had were the Bible, the Catechism, Watts' Psalms, and hymns and the almanacs."

"Well, then, what was the matter?" the historian persisted.

"Young man," Captain Preston replied, "what

we meant in going for those Redcoats was this: we always had been free, and we meant to be free always. They didn't mean we should."

Americans get this; we have for a long time. So why don't the Hollywood and media elite have a clue? There was a time when our popular culture shared the American people's admiration of our fighting men and women. They didn't just mouth words about "supporting the troops" while they trashed everything our soldiers were fighting for, the way they often do today. Even Hollywood celebrities risked their lives for the freedom that made them rich. During World War II, Jimmy Stewart was the number two male movie star at the box office when he enlisted in the U.S. Air Force Reserve. He flew twenty bombing missions and ended up a brigadier general. Henry Fonda distinguished himself from his daughter by serving in combat in the Pacific. Later, Elvis Presley interrupted his career as the reigning king of rock and roll to be drafted into the army.

The stories are legion. When he was already a famous director, John Ford joined the navy during World War II and put together a film crew made up of Hollywood writers, directors, and technicians to document the war. When he was filming the Battle of Midway from a perch on the top of a power station, he was knocked out by a piece of flying concrete. When he came to, he kept shooting. Then, when shrapnel tore a hole in his arm and he could no longer hold a camera, he kept relaying information on the incoming planes to the navy command.

Here's how Ford himself described the Midway battle in a debriefing with the navy:

By this time the attack had started in earnest. There was some dive bombing at objectives like water towers, [they] got the hangar right away. I was close to the hangar and I was lined up on it with my camera, figuring it would be one of the first things they got . . . A Zero flew about 50 feet over it and dropped a bomb and hit it, the whole thing went up. I was knocked unconscious. Just knocked me goofy for a bit, and I pulled myself out of it. I did manage to get the picture. You may have seen it in [the movie] "The Battle of Midway." It's where the plane flies over the hangar and everything goes up in smoke and debris, you can see one big chunk coming for the camera.

. . . The Marines with me—I took one look at them and I said, "Well this war was won." They were kids, oh, I would say from 18 to 22, none of them were older. They were the calmest people I have ever seen. They were up there popping away with rifles, having a swell time and none of them were alarmed. I mean the thing [a Japanese bomb] would drop through, they would laugh and say "My God that one was close." I figured then, *"Well, if these kids are American kids, I mean this war is practically won."* (emphasis mine)

Today, one Hollywood director, Steven Spielberg, has shown some of the same support for our military in movies like *Saving Private Ryan* and his TV miniseries *The Pacific.* But can you imagine any Hollywood types personally putting themselves on the line for freedom the way Stewart, Fonda, and Ford did? Today Hollywood seems to be more at home disparaging the war effort than supporting it. During the Iraq War, Hollywood did something it had never done before in the history of American warfare: It made movies like *Rendition* and *Green Zone*, films that were critical of the war while the troops were still fighting in the field. It's their right to be critical, of course, just as it's our right not to support undermining our troops while they're risking their lives in battle; and Americans didn't. These anti–Iraq War films all tanked at the box office. You would think that if love of country didn't inspire Hollywood to make different films, love of box office receipts would.

What makes this reflexive anti-Americanism hardest to swallow is the fact that it is our troops—these men and women who are being portrayed as unwitting (and witting) agents of greed and evil on the big screen—who make the entertainment industry possible. Hollywood stars like nothing better than to stand up on Oscar night and congratulate themselves for their courage in speaking truth to power. They forget—or refuse to acknowledge—that someone is paying the price for their freedom to speak their minds. Dissent may be a form of patriotism, but it's far from the highest form. Our men and women in uniform own that honor. I am reminded of a poem my uncle e-mailed me recently:

> It is the veteran, not the preacher, who has given us freedom of religion.
>
> It is the veteran, not the reporter, who has given us freedom of the press.
>
> It is the veteran, not the poet, who has given us freedom of speech.
>
> It is the veteran, not the campus organizer, who has given us freedom to assemble.
>
> It is the veteran, not the lawyer, who has given us the right to a fair trial.
>
> It is the veteran, not the politician, who has given us the right to vote.
>
> It is the veteran, who salutes the flag, who serves

under the flag, and whose coffin will be draped by the flag.

Not everyone in popular culture likes to run America down, of course. I particularly liked country singer Toby Keith's song, "Courtesy of the Red, White and Blue." Toby was inspired to write it by the events of September 11, and he wrote it in honor of his father, an army veteran who died just before the attack. At first he would sing it only at live performances for the troops. Then the commandant of the Marine Corps told him it was his duty as an American to record the song. So he did, and here's my favorite part:

> And you'll be sorry that you messed with
> The U S of A
> 'Cause we'll put a boot in your ass
> It's the American way

We ask a lot of our fighting men and women. We ask them to be away from their families for long stretches of time. We ask them to live in hellish conditions. We ask them to risk their lives. The least—the very least—we can do is support them in this mission. That doesn't mean never questioning a war or our leaders. It means understanding when fundamental principles are at stake, and acknowledging those who bear the burden of their defense. It means being able to say what Ronald Reagan said to the surviving "boys of Pointe du Hoc" on the fortieth anniversary of the D-day invasion:

> You all knew that some things are worth dying for. One's country is worth dying for, and democracy is worth dying for, because it's the most deeply honorable form of government ever devised by man. All of you loved liberty. All of you were willing to fight tyranny, and you knew the people of your countries were behind you.

Hollywood may have its version of our military, but most of the young men and women who are sacrificing for our ideals are people we've never heard of. They are ordinary Americans shouldering a tremendous burden.

It says something remarkable about the American people and not just our ideals that our country has survived and thrived as long as it has. We can and should celebrate the giants of America—the Washingtons, the Lincolns, and the Reagans. But for more than two hundred years the burden of protecting this remarkable country has fallen on ordinary Americans and their families.

When I was a kid, my mom collected copies of the *Reader's Digest* and kept them on a shelf in our living room. I used to love reading through the snippets of Americana in those compact magazines. One summer my family drove five thousand miles round trip to my dad's twenty-fifth high school reunion in Sandpoint, Idaho, in a 1969 blue Ford station wagon. All we had for entertainment was each other and a pile of *Reader's Digests*. We read many stories of the valor of our fighting men and women that summer.

I remember over the years reading an amazing story about Staff Sergeant Henry Erwin, a chunky, red-haired radio operator on a B-29 conducting raids on Japan from Guam during World War II. Sergeant Erwin was a soft-spoken guy with a Southern accent that his crewmates liked to tease him about. One night, on a routine squadron mission, Sergeant Erwin was in what they called a "pathfinder" plane—the plane that dropped a phosphorus smoke bomb to direct the formation before they reached the target. Sergeant Erwin's job was to release the phosphorus bomb through a narrow tube in the rear of the plane on a signal from the pilot.

But that night there was a malfunction. The phosphorus bomb—which burns so hotly it effortlessly melts metal—exploded in the tube. Instead of falling out of the plane, the bomb bounced back up onto Sergeant Erwin.

He was blinded in both eyes and had an ear seared off by the blast, but the radio operator knew he had a bigger problem. The phosphorus bomb was now at his feet and burning through the deck of the plane toward the full load of incendiaries on the racks below. Here's what Sergeant Erwin did next, as told to the author of the article by the pilot, Captain Tony Simeral:

There was no time to think. He picked up the white-hot bomb in his bare hands, and started forward to the cockpit, groping his way with elbows and feet.

The navigator's folding table was down and latched, blocking the narrow passageway. Erwin hugged the blazing bomb under an arm, feeling it devour the flesh on his ribs, unfastened the spring latch and lifted the table. (We inspected the plane later; the skin of his entire hand was seared onto the table.)

He stumbled on, a walking torch. His clothes, hair and flesh were ablaze.

The dense smoke had filled the airplane, and Simeral had opened the window beside him to clear the air. "I couldn't see Erwin," he told us, "but I heard his voice right at my elbow. He said"—Simeral paused a moment to steady his own voice. "He said, *'Pardon me, sir,'* and reached across to the window and tossed out the bomb. Then he collapsed on the flight deck." A fire extinguisher was turned on him, but the phosphorous still burned.

That very night, while Sergeant Erwin clung to life as he was treated for his burns, his superiors wrote up their recommendation for him to receive the Congressional Medal of Honor. Washington approved the honor in record time, but because there was no medal available on Guam, they had to send to Honolulu to find one. Sergeant Erwin's commanding general personally delivered the medal from Honolulu to Erwin's bedside in Guam. Everyone was happy they were able to honor the hero in time, but this modest man's actions to save his comrades spoke louder than any award ever could. I remember thinking that the title of the article said it all: "Sergeant Erwin and the Blazing Bomb: A Story of a Night When the Congressional Medal of Honor Seemed to Be a Modest Award."

I also read about a later war, the war in Vietnam. I remember one horrifying article that reported how Captain Chris O'Sullivan of Astoria, Queens, was killed in 1965 leading a counterattack against the Vietcong. The son of Irish immigrants, Chris O'Sullivan had grown up in a walk-up apartment above a candy store. Like so many immigrants, Chris's father had a special understanding of the gift that is American citizenship, and he instilled that appreciation in his son. Captain O'Sullivan served with bravery and distinction in Vietnam. But I read with heartbroken amazement how, after his death, his widow received anonymous phone calls saying "it was a good thing" her husband was killed in the war.

I'm grateful every day that Track and his fellow soldiers, sailors, airmen, and Marines live in a country that no longer looks down on their service. The treatment of servicemen and -women coming home from Vietnam—literally being spit on and called "baby killers"—is a dark and shameful chapter in our history. We can and often do disagree with the decisions made by the civilian and military leaders who command our young men and women. And we do become war weary. But the American people, to their everlasting credit, have no stomach for taking out our war weariness on the men and women who serve.

To the contrary, I meet Americans every day who are engaged in activities to honor and support our troops, whether it is baking cookies (Track and his buddies received them, by the way, and they send a hearty thanks!), knitting wool caps for those cold nights in Afghanistan, or just writing a letter every once in a while.

Just as important, Americans continue to support

our troops and their families after they come home, many of them with serious injuries. Todd and I have met with dozens of returning servicemen and -women, including those through the Wounded Warrior Project. We've visited Walter Reed Hospital to meet mighty warriors, and I've twice visited Landstuhl Regional Medical Center in Germany, where wounded troops from Iraq and Afghanistan receive treatment. We are forever grateful to the hundreds of Americans—many of whom have no personal connection to the warriors they care for—who haven't forgotten that our troops need our support even after they've left combat.

What may be most remarkable about our servicemen and -women is, whatever their reasons for serving, heroism isn't one of them.

I remember being on the campaign trail with John McCain and hearing people attack him in deeply personal ways and thinking, *Do they know that they are insulting a genuine American hero? Are they fit to tie his boots, much less take cheap shots at him?*

Most Americans are by now familiar with the outlines of the story of John's five and a half years of captivity in a North Vietnamese prisoner-of-war camp. We know about the torture he endured, the cruelty of his captors, and the love and camaraderie of the fellow Americans he was imprisoned with.

But what most Americans may not know is that John McCain doesn't consider himself a hero. Why? Because, under constant beatings and torture, and after repeatedly refusing to be released before Americans who had been imprisoned longer than he, John signed a confession written by his captors. Here is how he describes the scene in his wonderful memoir *Faith of My Fathers*:

At two- to three-hour intervals, the guards returned to administer beatings. The intensity of the punishment varied from visit to visit depending on the enthusiasm and energy of the guards. Still, I felt they were being careful not to kill or permanently injure me. One guard would hold me while the others pounded away. Most blows were directed at my shoulder, chest, and stomach. Occasionally, when I had fallen to the floor, they kicked me in the head. They cracked several of my ribs and broke a couple of teeth. My bad right leg was swollen and hurt the most of any of my injuries. Weakened by beatings and dysentery, and with my right leg again nearly useless, I found it almost impossible to stand.

On the third night, I lay in my own blood and waste, so tired and hurt that I could not move. The Prick [a prison guard] came in with two other guards, lifted me to my feet, and gave me the worst beating I had yet experienced. At one point he slammed his fist into my face and knocked me across the room toward the waste bucket. I fell on the bucket, hitting it with my left arm, and breaking it again. They left me lying on the floor, moaning from the stabbing pain in my refractured arm.

In hideous pain, John tried to take his own life, he goes on to describe, by using his shirt as a noose to hang himself. Thankfully, the guards saw him and stopped this remarkable American before he could be successful. The guards didn't do it out of any love for America, but they were nonetheless giving us a great gift. Soon after, however, came John's moment of reckoning:

On the fourth day, I gave up.

"I am a black criminal," the interrogator wrote, "and I have performed the deeds of an air pirate. I almost died and the Vietnamese people saved my life. The doctors gave me an operation that I did not deserve."

I had been taken back to the theater after telling the guards I was ready to confess. For twelve hours I had written out many drafts of the confession. I used words that I hoped would discredit its authenticity, and I tried to keep it in stilted generalities and Communist jargon so that it would be apparent that I had signed it under duress.

The interrogator had edited my last draft and decided to rewrite most of it himself. He then handed it to me and told me to copy it out in my own hand. I started to print it in block letters, and he ordered me to write in script. He demanded that I add an admission that I had bombed a school. I refused, and we argued back and forth about the confession's contents for a time before I gave in to his demand. Finally, they took me to sign the document.

They took me back to my room and let me sleep through the night. The next morning, they brought me back to the theater and ordered me to record my confession on tape. I refused, and was beaten until I consented.

I was returned to my cell and left alone for the next two weeks.

They were the worst two weeks of my life. I couldn't rationalize away my confession. I was ashamed. I felt faithless, and couldn't control my despair. I shook, as if my disgrace were a fever. I kept imagining that they would release my confession to embarrass my father. All my pride was lost, and I doubted I would ever stand up to any man again. Nothing could save me. No one would ever look upon me again with anything but pity or contempt.

From the comfort of my life of safety and security in Wasilla, it is impossible for me to truly understand how John endured what he did, much less how he could feel shame for breaking under the cruelty of his captors. But such is the remarkable character of this man and the men and women of our armed forces. So many voices try to subtly paint these young men and women as too stupid to know what's good for them; to portray them as people, in Senator John Kerry's words, who have failed to get an education and are therefore "stuck in Iraq." But our military men and women are made of stronger stuff than these critics can ever imagine. They defend their critics' right to bad-mouth them and they don't complain. They protect our very freedom and don't consider themselves heroes.

I wonder if this irony ever dawns on the self-described truth tellers of Washington, the mainstream media, Hollywood, and academia: all of the values they hold dear—their ability to speak freely, to criticize and caricature the military, to demonize Christianity and America's traditional values—mean nothing unless they are defended by these courageous men and women.

The same is true for all of us. Washington politicians talk in lofty tones about their love of liberty, and many of us outside of Washington do, too. After all, freedom has brought us tremendous opportunity and prosperity in America. But what does it mean to simply say we love freedom? Every so often—too often, unfortunately— freedom has to be fought for. It has to be defended or else it's just an empty word.

I remember at Iditarod Elementary School, in the early 1970s, my big brother's sixth-grade choir (which hadn't yet been taken over by the politically correct police) sang "Freedom Isn't Free." I listened intently as the young baritones, under the direction of Mr. Kraus's baton, sang:

"Freedom isn't free. You've got to pay the price. You've got to sacrifice, for our liberty."

All these years, these lyrics have stayed with me. And thanks to heroes like John McCain, they're more than just words.

One of the last stops on my *Going Rogue* book tour was at Fort Hood, Texas, in early December 2009. Less than a month earlier, on November 5, an American military psychiatrist who had become a jihadist opened fire in a military clinic on base. Before he was taken down by police, he managed to kill thirteen of his fellow soldiers and wound dozens more.

When Todd and I visited Fort Hood, the base was still raw with the wounds of November 5, 2009. Thanks to the generosity of *Going Rogue* readers, we were able to donate thousands of dollars to the families of servicemen and -women killed and wounded in the attack.

Just before my visit, my brother sent me a description of the American military man that I think is spot-on—with the exception that it doesn't include American military women. I don't know who wrote it, but the attributes it describes apply to both sexes equally:

> The average age of the military man is nineteen years. He is a short-haired, tight-muscled kid who, under normal circumstances is considered by society as half man, half boy. Not yet dry behind the ears, not old enough to buy a beer, but old enough to die for his country. He never really cared much for work and he would rather wax his own car than wash his father's, but he has never collected unemployment either.
>
> He's a recent high school graduate; he was

probably an average student, pursued some form of sport activities, drives a ten-year-old jalopy, and has a steady girlfriend that either broke up with him when he left or swears to be waiting when he returns from half a world away. He listens to rock and roll or hip-hop or rap or jazz or swing and a 155mm howitzer.

He is ten or fifteen pounds lighter now than when he was at home because he is working or fighting from before dawn to well after dusk. He has trouble spelling, thus letter writing is a pain for him, but he can field strip a rifle in thirty seconds and reassemble it in less time in the dark. He can recite to you the nomenclature of a machine gun or grenade launcher and use either one effectively if he must.

He digs foxholes and latrines and can apply first aid like a professional.

He can march until he is told to stop, or stop until he is told to march.

He obeys orders instantly and without hesitation, but he is not without spirit or individual dignity. He is self-sufficient.

He has two sets of fatigues: he washes one and wears the other. He keeps his canteens full and his feet dry.

He sometimes forgets to brush his teeth, but never to clean his rifle. He can cook his own meals, mend his own clothes, and fix his own hurts.

If you're thirsty, he'll share his water with you; if you are hungry, his food. He'll even split his ammunition with you in the midst of battle when you run low.

He has learned to use his hands like weapons and weapons like they were his hands.

He can save your life—or take it, because that is his job. He will often do twice the work of a civilian, draw half the pay, and still find ironic humor in it all. He has seen more suffering and death than he should have in his short lifetime. He has wept in public and in private, for friends who have fallen in combat and is unashamed.

He feels every note of the National Anthem vibrate through his body while at rigid attention, while tempering the burning desire to "square-away" those around him who haven't bothered to stand, remove their hat, or even stop talking.

In an odd twist, day in and day out, far from home, he defends their right to be disrespectful.

Just as did his father, grandfather, and great-grandfather, he is paying the price for our freedom. Beardless or not, he is not a boy. He is the American Fighting Man that has kept this country free for over two hundred years.

He has asked nothing in return, except our friendship and understanding.

Remember him, always, for he has earned our respect and admiration with his blood.

And now we even have women over there in danger, doing their part in this tradition of going to war when our nation calls us to do so.

As you go to bed tonight, remember this. A short lull, a little shade, and a picture of loved ones in their helmets.

Some might think this description is overly sentimental, and maybe it is. But since my brother sent this to me, countless military families have recommended it to me and I've seen it on dozens of military websites.

Our military families are justifiably proud of their husbands and wives and sons and daughters who are serving. But they're not naïve. Military families see war close up. They're not easily swayed by propaganda, be it pro or con. They know the reality of sacrifice, not the theory.

Call me biased, but as the mom of a U.S. Army combat vet, I know that our military families sacrifice alongside our military men and women. They don't personally experience the danger and the harsh conditions, but they know someone they love is experiencing them. For weeks and months at a time, they often don't even know where their loved one is, or if he or she is all right. For them, time is measured in the units between receiving those letters and those phone calls. Believe me, I know. The year Track was deployed in Iraq was an eventful year for me, to say the least. I went through a tough presidential campaign and then came home to a transformed—and hyper-partisan—political environment in Alaska. But throughout that challenging year, the days I heard from Track were days when no one and nothing could touch me. Todd and I would think, *Okay, Associated Press,* New York Times*: Write what you want. Take your best shot. It doesn't matter. We heard from our son today and he's okay. Nothing else matters.*

During the year they spent in the Diyala Province, the Stryker Brigade lost many soldiers. Many souls went home. Many families grieved.

The more than three thousand members who made it back home have returned to their base in Alaska. Like Track, they are figuring out how and where to finish their military obligations. The possibility that they will be redeployed as active-duty members or national guardsmen—maybe to Afghanistan this time—is very real.

In the end, the question of why these young men and women serve is probably best answered by us, not them. The lost soldiers from the Stryker Brigade can no longer tell us why they made the ultimate sacrifice. But more important than their motives is our recognition that they died to preserve something great. And more important than our words of gratitude—however heartfelt they are—are our actions. Abraham Lincoln said it for all time on the battlefield at Gettysburg: "The world will little note nor long remember what we say here, but it can never forget what they did here. It is for us the living rather to be dedicated here to the unfinished work which they who fought here have thus far so nobly advanced."

Our military men and women fight—and die—to defend our freedom. They do their duty. But we have a duty as well. Our duty is to cherish the great gift they have given us; to honor their service and their memory by preserving what Lincoln so memorably called "government of the people, by the people and for the people."

If you ever have the chance to come to Washington, don't miss visiting Arlington National Cemetery. For me, there is no more powerful reminder of the responsibility we all have to the men and women memorialized by the acres of white markers. As the poet Karl Shapiro reminds us in his poem "Elegy for a Dead Soldier," as long as we breathe free, we know the reason for their service—and their sacrifice.

> Underneath this wooden cross there lies
> A Christian killed in battle. You who read
> Remember that this stranger died in pain;
> And passing here, if you can lift your eyes
> Upon a peace kept by human creed
> Know that one soldier has not died in vain.

Three

AMERICA THE EXCEPTIONAL

There is a depressing predictability to conversations about America these days. More times than not, if you try to say something nice about our country, you're accused of being a closed-minded nativist, one of those dangerous hicks clinging to her guns, her God, and her country. The equally unpleasant corollary to this practice is that America's critics never seem to give her the benefit of the doubt anymore. She's never merely wrong in their eyes; she's just plain bad.

I was reminded of this distasteful tendency when

Arizona recently passed a law that allows state law enforcement officers to question suspected lawbreakers about their immigration status. Love the law or hate the law, you couldn't help but notice that the reception it received from its critics seemed designed not just to discredit the statute, but to cast America itself in the most negative possible light. If you relied on MSNBC for your news, suddenly Arizona—and, by extension, all of red-state America—had become the equivalent of Nazi Germany. Even worse was the way the law was portrayed by those who should have known better—including members of the Obama administration and others in Washington—as a sign of the inherent badness of America.

As soon as the Arizona law was passed, the Obama administration shifted into a familiar mode: Apologizing for America before foreign audiences. In talks with Chinese officials (representatives of a regime that kills and jails political dissidents and forces abortions on women, among its many other human rights abuses), State Department officials called the Arizona law part of a "troubling trend in our society and an indication that we have to deal with issues of discrimination." Many members of Congress even shamefully stood and applauded when Mexican president Felipe Calderón spoke before a joint session of Congress and accused Arizona of using "racial profiling as a basis for law enforcement." This, from a head of state whose law enforcement officials have repeatedly been accused of turning a blind eye to human rights abuses of immigrants on its southern border and does more to encourage illegal immigration to the United States than to see that Mexican citizens can provide for their families by working in their homeland.

The knee-jerk tendency on the part of some to run down America and accuse her fans of being mindless hillbillies is getting old. On the other hand, I'm not interested in closing my eyes to our country's problems. There has to be a middle ground, a way of talking about America that shows we are proud of her greatness but not blind to her flaws. Of course, we're not perfect, and the accusation that anyone who chooses to accentuate America's positive aspects is claiming that we are without blemish is not just tiresome but hurtful. It's a way of keeping the conversation focused on our flaws. It's a game of "gotcha" played by people who are either too disdainful of or too insecure about America's beauty to handle an honest conversation about our country.

You've probably heard a term being used by those who believe America is a special nation with a special role in the world: *American exceptionalism.* It may sound kind of cocky and arrogant to some people. But what do we mean when we say America is an exceptional country? We're not saying we're better than anyone else, or that we have the right to tell people in other countries how to live their lives. When we say America is exceptional we're saying we are the lucky heirs to a unique set of beliefs and national qualities, and that we need to preserve and value those beliefs. We're saying America is a model to the world, not a bully to the world, or responsible *for* the world.

In one of my favorite magazines, *National Review*, Richard Lowry and Ramesh Ponnuru explain America's special character well:

> Our country has always been exceptional. It is freer, more individualistic, more democratic, and more open and dynamic than any other nation on earth. These qualities are the bequest of our Founding and of our cultural heritage. They have always marked America as special, with a unique role and mission in the world: as a model of ordered liberty and self-government and as an exemplar of freedom and a vindicator of it, through persuasion when possible and force of arms when absolutely necessary.

The idea of American exceptionalism is older than the United States itself. When Ronald Reagan used to speak of a "shining city on a hill," he was borrowing from John Winthrop, a preacher who led a group of Puritans to religious freedom in America in 1630.

"We shall be as a city upon a hill. The eyes of all people are upon us."

Winthrop, in turn, was borrowing from Matthew 5:14, in which Jesus tells his followers, "You are the light of the world. A city that is set on a hill cannot be hidden."

"The light of the world." "A city on a hill." These are high aspirations for a people in a strange new land. And it's one of the more curious things about American history, I've learned, that it was the Frenchman Alexis de Tocqueville who described how America has managed to mostly fulfill this promise. If you pay attention while you're listening to C-SPAN or reading American history you're sure to come across Tocqueville. He literally wrote the book on American exceptionalism.

In 1831, Tocqueville spent nine months traveling from Boston to Michigan to New Orleans trying to find out about this thing called democracy in this place called America. The first volume of his book, appropriately titled *Democracy in America*, was published in 1835 and was an instant success. What he saw in America was a country and a people distinctly different from Europe, and thus exceptional. Tocqueville said that three things—American customs (particularly our religious heritage), law (particularly our commitment to federalism, or states' rights), and geography combined to make "the position of the Americans . . . quite exceptional, and it may be believed that no democratic people will ever be placed in a similar one."

One aspect of American exceptionalism as described by Alexis de Tocqueville that is particularly meaningful today is our propensity to govern ourselves, locally, without waiting for any central authority to show us the way. He could have been talking about towns I've been to in New Jersey, Ohio, Texas, or Alaska, for that matter, when he wrote, "In towns it is impossible to prevent men from assembling, getting excited together and forming sudden passionate resolves. Towns are like great meeting houses with all the inhabitants as members. In them the people wield immense influence over their magistrates and often carry their desires into execution without intermediaries."

Tocqueville's vision of an exceptional system of government combining with an exceptional people to produce an exceptional country is echoed in the writings of American scholars today. Sociologist Charles Murray explains that even though other countries oftentimes don't like to admit it, they, too, know there is something different about America:

American exceptionalism is not just something that Americans claim for themselves. Historically, Americans have been different as a people, even peculiar, and everyone around the world has recognized it. I'm thinking of qualities such as American optimism even when there doesn't seem to be any good reason for it. That's quite uncommon among the peoples of the world. There is the striking lack of class envy in America—by and large, Americans celebrate others' success instead of resenting it. That's just about unique, certainly compared to European countries, and something that drives European intellectuals crazy. And then there is perhaps the most important symptom of all, the signature of American exceptionalism—the assumption by most Americans that they are in control of their own destinies. It is hard to think of a more inspiriting quality for a population to possess, and the American population still possesses it to an astonishing degree. No other country comes close.

Remembering that humility is a virtue, we recognize and value what makes America unique, but that doesn't give us an excuse to be boastful. Neither, though, does it demand that we owe the world an apology for our success and our leadership. What so many on the left don't want to admit is that America has been a force for good, not simply for her own people, but for the world. It is a mystery to me why this is so difficult for some to admit. But these days, it's like a breath of fresh air when you hear a leader straightforwardly and unapologetically state the facts of American greatness. I came across a recently published letter from (who else?) Ronald Reagan to then–Soviet premier Leonid Brezhnev that does just that. It was written when Reagan had just gotten out of the hospital following the 1981 assassination attempt. His presidency was just weeks old. In his letter, written in his own hand in response to what he characterized as a letter of "somewhat intemperate" tone from the Soviet leader, President Reagan made it clear that America would not apologize for its leadership in the world:

> Is it possible that we have let ideology, political and economical philosophy and governmental policies keep us from considering the very real, everyday problems of the people we represent? Will the average Russian family be better off or even aware that his government has imposed a government of its liking on the people of Afghanistan? . . .
>
> In your letter you imply that such things have

been made necessary because of territorial ambitions of the United States; that we have imperialistic designs and thus constitute a threat to your own security and that of the newly emerging nations. There not only is no evidence to support such a charge, there is solid evidence that the United States when it could have dominated the world with no risk to itself made no effort whatsoever to do so.

When WWII ended the United States had the only undamaged industrial power in the world. Its military might was at its peak—and we alone had the ultimate weapon, the nuclear bomb with the unquestioned ability to deliver it anywhere in the world. If we had sought world domination who could have opposed us? But the United States followed a different course—one unique in all the history of mankind. We used our power and wealth to rebuild the war-ravaged economies of all the world including those nations who had been our enemies.

Read that, and tell me you're not proud to be an American!

Sad to say, many of our national leaders no longer believe in American exceptionalism. They—perhaps dearly—love their country and want what's best for it, but they think America is just an ordinary nation and so America should act like just an ordinary nation. They don't believe we have a special message for the world or a special mission to preserve our greatness for the betterment of not just ourselves but all of humanity. Astonishingly, President Obama even said that he believes in American exceptionalism in the same way "the Brits believe in British exceptionalism and the Greeks believe in Greek exceptionalism." Which is to say, he doesn't believe in American exceptionalism at all. He seems to think it is just a kind of irrational prejudice in favor of our way of life. To me, that is appalling.

His statement reminds me of that great scene in the movie *The Incredibles*. Dash, the son in the superhero family, who is a super-fast runner, wants to try out for the track team at school. His mom claims it won't be fair. "Dad always said our powers were nothing to be ashamed of. Our powers made us special!" Dash objects. When his mom answers with the politically correct rejoinder "Everyone's special, Dash," Dash mutters, "Which is another way of saying no one is."

Maybe President Obama grew up around coaches who insisted that all the players receive participation "trophies" at the end of the season and where no score was kept in youth soccer games for fear of offending someone. Because just like Mrs. Incredible, when President Obama insists that all countries are exceptional, he's saying that none is, least of all the country he leads. That's a shame, because American exceptionalism is something that people in both parties used to believe in.

I recently reread for the first time in a long time President John F. Kennedy's inspiring inauguration speech. When you read the speech, the fact that Kennedy believed America is a nation unlike any other jumps off the page at you. President Kennedy never uses the term *American exceptionalism*, but his view of America as a place with a meaning and a mission of redemption is unmistakable:

> We observe today not a victory of party, but a celebration of freedom—symbolizing an end, as well as a beginning—signifying renewal, as well as change. For I have sworn before you and Almighty God the same solemn oath our forebears prescribed nearly a century and three quarters ago.
>
> The world is very different now. For man holds in his mortal hands the power to abolish all forms of human poverty and all forms of human life. And yet the same revolutionary beliefs for which our forebears fought are still at issue around the

globe—the belief that the rights of man come not from the generosity of the state, but from the hand of God.

We dare not forget today that we are the heirs of that first revolution. Let the word go forth from this time and place, to friend and foe alike, that the torch has been passed to a new generation of Americans—born in this century, tempered by war, disciplined by a hard and bitter peace, proud of our ancient heritage—and unwilling to witness or permit the slow undoing of those human rights to which this Nation has always been committed, and to which we are committed today at home and around the world.

It's hard to imagine a Democrat president voicing these sentiments today. Harder still, imagine him or her *meaning* them. Too often we hear from the left a different spin on American exceptionalism—a view that America is somehow worse than other countries, that it is hypocritical about its ideals, falls short of its responsibilities, and is forever in need of correction. This has been the main thrust of President Obama's speeches on the world stage since assuming office in January 2009.

I think ordinary Americans are tired of Obama's global apology tour and of hearing about what a weak country America is from left-wing professors and journalists. That's why America yearns for a return to national leadership of the kind exemplified by Presidents Reagan and Kennedy: leaders who are not embarrassed by America, who see our country's flaws but also its greatness; leaders who are proud to be Americans, and are proud of her every day, not just when their chosen ones are winning elections.

What makes America exceptional? The answer certainly begins with the American values of individual freedom and equality before the law that we've already discussed. The historic gift of our founding set the stage for our exceptionalism as a country, but it has been the American people putting that heritage to work by raising our families, building our communities, creating our prosperity, and defending our freedom that has truly made our country special.

As an Alaskan, I've always believed that one of the keys to American exceptionalism is a part of the Constitution we've touched on but haven't fully discussed yet: the Tenth Amendment. Here's how it reads:

The powers not delegated to the United States by the Constitution, nor prohibited by it to the States, are reserved to the States respectively, or to the people.

Nothing could be more simple and straightforward. There, in a single sentence, is the entire spirit of the U.S. Constitution: The federal government's powers are limited to those listed in the Constitution. Everything else belongs to the states and the people. We give you the power; you don't give us the power. We are sovereign.

In practice, I've always interpreted the Tenth Amendment to mean that the best government is government that is closest to the people. We Alaskans have good reason to believe in this principle. Much of the motivation for the drive for statehood back in the late 1950s was because of the way the feds ran the territory from Washington, D.C. Without representation in Congress, and all the things that statehood affords, there were laws made by the other states that hindered Alaska's development. For instance, when Alaska was just a territory, a law was passed called the Jones Act, which requires that goods shipped between U.S. ports be carried in U.S. vessels. This restriction has greatly increased the cost of goods from the Lower 48 for Alaskans.

This experience of being ruled by elites in a distant capital—in violation of both the spirit of the Tenth Amendment and Tocqueville's observation that our preference for local self-government is a crucial part of our exceptionalism—has had a lasting impact on my career in public service.

There's an excellent speech that Ernest Gruening, a Democrat who was a territorial governor of Alaska and a U.S. senator, gave at the Alaska Constitutional Convention in 1955 that is relevant for the whole country today. Gruening laid a foundation that many public servants, myself included, could build upon in our quest for maximum self-determination. His speech compared Alaska's fight for statehood to America's fight for independence. Gruening made the case that Alaska's rule (and taxation!) by Washington without representation was akin to "colonialism" and that it had to end.

For our nation was born of revolt against colonialism. Our charters of liberty—the Declaration of Independence and the Constitution—embody America's opposition to colonialism and to colonialism's inevitable abuses. It is therefore natural and proper that American leadership should set its face against the absenteeism, the discriminations and the oppressions of colonialism. It is natural and proper that American leadership should lend such aid and comfort as it may to other peoples striving for self-determination and for that univer-

sally applicable tenet of American faith—
government by consent of the governed.

Those Alaskans who fought for statehood were kin-
dred spirits in some ways to our nation's Founding Fathers because, like our Founders, they had their own
"fight" for independence from a remote power.

And isn't that basically what many Americans are
doing today? We're demanding to be heard by a remote
power in Washington that seems to ignore our wishes
as it thwarts the will of the people with Obamacare,
private-sector-industry takeovers, a lack of law enforcement on our porous borders, deficit spending, and
debt accumulation.

Not just Alaska, of course, but every state in the
union has a unique history, people, and perspective.
The thing that makes this all work—that brings all of
it together to unify a nation—is the spirit of the Tenth
Amendment. It's this principle that restrains government and maximizes freedom, allowing a diverse country not just to survive, but to thrive. Thomas Jefferson
put it this way in 1791, just as the Bill of Rights was
being ratified:

I consider the foundation of the Constitution as
laid on this ground: That "all powers not delegated to the United States, by the Constitution, nor

prohibited by it to the States, are reserved to the States or to the people." *To take a single step beyond the boundaries thus specially drawn around the powers of Congress, is to take possession of a boundless field of power, no longer susceptible of any definition.* (emphasis mine)

A "boundless field of power"—sounds like it could be a description of the current flood of legislation coming out of Washington. What we're seeing today is the inevitable result of national leaders who have forgotten the fundamental wisdom of the Tenth Amendment. Just as Mr. Jefferson warned us, as soon as we as a country disregarded the fact that the federal government's powers are limited, and that we as states and individuals hold the balance of the power, the floodgates were opened to the torrent of federal power grabs we're seeing today. Take the federal income tax, for example. We tend to think there are two constants in life: death and taxes. But America hasn't always had an income tax. The first federal income tax on individuals was imposed in 1861 to help pay for the Civil War. But the tax was never meant to be permanent, and Congress repealed it ten years after it was enacted. It wasn't until 1913 that the Sixteenth Amendment to the Constitution was ratified and the individual federal income tax that we know today was created.

What is most dangerous about these power grabs is that they're usually done in the name of a good cause—insuring the uninsured, for example—and have a big wad of cash attached to them.

The Obama administration's mammoth $787 billion stimulus package is a good example of this tactic of bribing the states to surrender their rights. As governor of Alaska, I angered a lot of state bureaucrats and their allies in Juneau when I turned down a chunk of the federal money slated for Alaska in Obama's stimulus bill. I accepted the money that would go to create real private-sector jobs through construction projects and provide needed medical care to the disadvantaged, but I said "no, thank you" to dollars that had fat federal strings attached to them. The Alaska legislature warned me they would join with other states led by conservative governors and find a way through litigation to go around the governor's office to accept the federal funds. But I stuck to my guns because the cost to our Tenth Amendment freedom was just too high. Not just in Alaska but in every state of the union, the debt-ridden, unsustainable stimulus scheme disrespected the Tenth Amendment by attempting to bribe the states with money in exchange for more Washington control. The money would have gone to fund government, not real jobs in the private sector. Embarrassingly, the Republican-controlled state legislature overrode my veto and Alaska accepted the funds. And now, to pay for them, Alaskans will have to put up with even more rule making from Washington.

I wasn't alone in my concern that the American people and the states were being had with the stimulus bill. I remember logging on to the Internet one day after those "Project Funded by the American Recovery and Reinvestment Act" signs began appearing all over the place. I guess the point of those signs was to make us grateful for the federal dollars Washington has decided to "give" us, as if we didn't understand that every dollar spent by Washington is a dollar that comes from us, the taxpayers, in the first place. Anyway, I logged on to a favorite website and found an interesting and hilarious "Photo of the Day." Someone in Henry County, Georgia, had decided to have a little fun (and make an important point) with one of those signs by plastering a copy of the Tenth Amendment on it. Big, red block letters underneath the text of the amendment read, "POWER IS GIVEN, NOT TAKEN."

The notion of states defending their power and independence under the Tenth Amendment has taken a beating in recent years. Advocates of bigger government have labored long and hard to equate any notion of "states' rights" with the racists who evoked this cause to defend segregation during the civil rights struggle. Ending discrimination against African Americans by some American states was one instance in which the federal government rightly stepped in and forced change. But since then, advocates of increased federal authority have abused this noble cause to advance a big-government agenda. Unfunded mandates in the form of environmental regulations and the Obamacare individual health insurance mandate have rained down on the states. And rules on everything from the gas we emit to the doctors we can choose have poured out of the nation's capital. In the process, America has come to be less a federal republic than a fifty-state colony of Washington, D.C.

We've lost the commonsense notion that helped make us great: that, in simple terms, we are all grown-ups and deserve to be treated as such. Hard as it is to believe, this used to be a pretty popular sentiment in America. In an old issue of the magazine *The Freeman,* I found the text of a resolution adopted by the Indiana state legislature in 1947, after the scope of the federal government had grown exponentially during World War II and Franklin Roosevelt's New Deal. The words of this short resolution show a spark of independence and self-sufficiency that desperately needs rekindling today:

Indiana needs no guardian and intends to have none. We Hoosiers—like the people of our sister states—were fooled for quite a spell with the magician's trick that a dollar taxed out of our pockets and sent to Washington will be bigger when it comes back to us. We have taken a good look at said dollar. We find that it lost weight in its journey to Washington and back. The political brokerage of the bureaucrats has been deducted. We have decided that here is no such thing as "federal" aid. We know that there is no wealth to tax that is not already within the boundaries of the forty-eight states.

So we propose henceforth to tax ourselves and take care of ourselves. We are fed up with subsidies, doles, and paternalism. We are no one's stepchild. We have grown up. We serve notice that we will resist Washington, DC adopting us.

Be it resolved by the House of Representatives of the General Assembly of the State of Indiana, the Senate concurring: That we respectfully petition and urge Indiana's congressmen and senators to vote to fetch our county courthouse and city halls back from Pennsylvania Avenue. We want government to come home. *Resolved further,* that we call upon the legislatures of our *sister states* and on *good citizens everywhere* who believe in the basic principles of Lincoln and Jefferson to join with us, and we with them to restore the American Republic and our forty-eight states to the foundations built by our fathers.

In a speech in Indiana as president in 1982, Ronald Reagan noted that, by 1951, Congress still hadn't acted on this resolution, so the Indiana state legislature passed another one. This one said: "We Hoosiers believe that the historic constitutional rights and responsibilities of the States must be recovered; that the tax sources of which we have been deprived must be restored; and that the Federal Government must restrict its activities to matters of the broadest national interest." To which Reagan quipped, "Well, it's taken over thirty years, but, I'm happy to report, your message has finally gotten through. To tell you the truth, I believed you the first time you said it."

Only Ronald Reagan could make a joke of what so many try to portray as dangerous radicalism. But the sentiments expressed by the Indiana legislators aren't radicalism, they're common sense, or at least what used to be recognized as common sense: "We know that there is no wealth to tax that is not already within the boundaries of the forty-eight states." Substitute "fifty states" for "forty-eight" and you have a rallying cry for today.

We are no one's stepchild. We have grown up. We

serve notice that we will resist Washington, D.C., adopting us.

Another aspect of American exceptionalism we are in danger of losing today is our belief in free markets and good old-fashioned American hard work and ingenuity. Particularly in the aftermath of the recent financial crisis, we hear a lot about how America needs to become more like Europe, with free health care, a month of paid vacation every year, cradle-to-grave government benefits—and the permanent double-digit unemployment and bankrupt national treasuries that go along with it. Unbelievably, at a time when countries such as Greece, Portugal, and Spain are going broke, the current administration wants us to become more like them, not less.

This is another example of the gaping disconnect between the utopian schemes of the self-proclaimed elite and the wisdom of the American people. America is and always has been a nation of strivers—people who want not just to get by but to get ahead. Our prosperity has always depended on the fact that we've had the economic freedom to pursue our dreams. It's one of the reasons why the sort of attempts at class warfare that work so well in Europe—pitting the less financially well off against the better off—don't usually work in

America. We all want to be better off. We want a better life for our children and grandchildren and we know that working hard and taking advantage of opportunities when they present themselves are the way to do it.

Wisconsin congressional representative Paul Ryan said it best: "Americans don't want a government that says, 'This is your lot in life. Accept it and we'll help you cope with it.' Americans want a government that allows them to seek a *better* lot in life." We can and should provide a safety net for those who stumble and fall. But we want the freedom to succeed, not the excuse never to have to try. We believe passionately that Abraham Lincoln was right when he said, "The man who labored for another last year, this year labors for himself, and next year will hire others to labor for him." That's the American dream.

This is a dream that has lifted more people out of poverty, made more millionaires, and produced more innovation than any other in history. It's a dream that doesn't discriminate on the basis of race, creed, or gender. It is open to all who want to work hard and take a chance.

Our history is full of examples of how hard work, entrepreneurialism, and economic freedom came together to produce miracles. One of the most inspiring to me personally is that of Chris Gardner, whose story was told in the remarkable film *The Pursuit of Happyness*, starring Will Smith.

I defy you to watch this movie without first crying and then shouting for joy. It is the story of a man who had a dream to fulfill and a responsibility to uphold in the form of his young son. Destitute and on the brink of homelessness, Gardner accepts sole custody of his son, even though the flophouse he is living in won't accept kids. The movie tells the story of Gardner's relentless fight to succeed—to pursue "happiness"—while fighting just as hard to take care of his son. The two were secretly homeless while Gardner went to work in a low-paying stock broker training program. He struggled to find a place for them to sleep each night, even resorting to finding shelter in a locked bathroom in the San Francisco train station. Meanwhile, he went to work every day to build a better life for both of them. He never gave up on his dream and he never left his son. Today, he is a successful businessman, motivational speaker, and philanthropist.

My husband, Todd, sums up the spirit of initiative and hard work behind the American dream when he repeats to our children the old adage: "God helps those who help themselves."

As for myself, I have a dog-eared copy of a quote on my bulletin board from David Sarnoff, the visionary founder of NBC, that has followed me from the Wasilla City Council chambers to the mayor's office to the Alaska Oil and Gas Conservation Commission and then to the Governor's Mansion:

Remember: nobody owes you a living.

Don't be misled into believing that somehow the world owes you a living. The boy who believes that his parents, or the government, or anyone else owes him his livelihood and that he can collect it without labor will wake up one day and find himself working for another boy who did not have that belief and, therefore, earned the right to have others work for him.

When human perseverance is combined with economic freedom, anything can happen. Miracles like Chris Gardner happen. At the heart of the American dream is the belief that anybody can succeed. We can, and do, fail as well. But we can brush ourselves off, get back up, and try to succeed again. No one but we determines who wins and who loses, how hard we work and how hard we try.

Since the financial crisis left so many of our pensions and IRAs in tatters, and so many Americans either looking for work or struggling to hang on to the jobs they have, there is no doubt that we need reform in part of our economy. But the federal government today is going further than just leveling the playing field for Americans who want to work hard and compete to get ahead. Government is now picking winners and losers.

Through the purchase of large chunks of Chrysler and General Motors, the bailing out of Wall Street banks, and putting union cronies ahead of other creditors in bankruptcies, government is taking over more and more of the role that the free market has traditionally played in America. The problem is that when government is calling the shots, it's politics that matters, not good ideas, hard work, or perseverance.

It's called crony capitalism, and it's something I fought against as governor. In Alaska, we took on "Big Oil" and its allies in government who were taking the forty-ninth state for a ride. My administration challenged lax rules that allowed corruption and irresponsible resource development, and we even took on the largest corporation in the world at the time, Exxon Mobil. The state argued that it was not abiding by provisions in contracts it held with Alaska. When it came time to craft a plan for a natural gas pipeline, we insisted on transparency and a level playing field to ensure fair competition. Our reforms helped reduce politicians' ability to play favorites and helped clean up corruption. "Big Oil," including executives and lobby-ists of BP, Exxon, ConocoPhillips, and others, didn't pal around with me, but, then, that was a mutual deci-sion.

Exactly the opposite is happening in Washington today as government burrows deeper into the Ameri-can economy. It's a vicious cycle. The more industries government owns, controls, and/or regulates, the more lobbyists these industries send to Capitol Hill. Inevi-tably, it's the lobbyists who are at the table when the legislation or the regulations that affect their employers are being crafted. Before you know it, you have health care and pharmaceutical lobbyists cutting deals to ben-efit their industries under the guise of "reform." Philip Morris shapes tobacco regulation. General Motors, BP, and other companies go along with job-killing "cap and trade" energy tax legislation in exchange for big subsi-dies for their products—the "green" ones government wants them to produce. The big corporations—the ones who can afford armies of lobbyists in Washington—win. We little guys lose.

Don't get me wrong: I'm as angry at the Wall Street "fat cats" (in the words of our president) who have done so much to undermine our economy—and escaped so many of the consequences—as the next gal. But the answer isn't to lose sight of the free market principles that have made America both the most prosperous and the most generous nation on earth.

Luigi Zingales, an economist at the University of Chicago, has perhaps done more than any other academic to warn us not to throw the baby out with the bathwater when it comes to our economy. Professor Zingales makes the crucial point that there is a difference between being pro-market and being probusiness. Both political parties are at fault in failing to acknowledge this distinction. Our government should seek to promote free and open markets, not pick winners and losers among different businesses. To do otherwise, the economist warns:

> is the path to big-business capitalism: a path that blurs the distinction between pro-market and probusiness policies, and so imperils the unique faith the American people have long displayed in the legitimacy of democratic capitalism.

Unfortunately, it looks for now like the Obama administration has chosen this latter path. It is a choice that threatens to launch us on that vicious spiral of more public resentment and more corporatist crony capitalism so common abroad—trampling in the process the economic exceptionalism that has been so crucial for American prosperity. When the dust has cleared and the panic has abated, this may well turn out to be the most serious and damaging consequence of the financial crisis for American capitalism.

The justification that supporters of greater government intervention in our economy use is that free market capitalism, left to itself, is unfair. As any poor, misguided viewer of Michael Moore's movies "knows," capitalists are greedy and self-interested. Government must therefore step in to regulate the free market in order to ensure a fair outcome.

This argument has been around for a long time. I remember back when I was studying the American economy in my high school history class, the late economist Milton Friedman had won the Nobel Prize in economics a few years earlier and he was all the rage. I wish he and his wife, Rose, were still with us today to defend free market principles from the likes of Michael Moore. In their many writings, they provided a powerful answer to the argument that government is necessary to get people to cooperate together for the greater good.

One of my favorite examples is also the simplest. In their fantastic television show *Free to Choose* (and their book by the same name), the Friedmans use a wonderful essay about the making of a pencil to illustrate the power of human economic freedom—and the damage government can do when it steps in to replace the collective energy and decision making of free individuals.

The essay "I, Pencil," by Leonard Read, explains how thousands of people—from those who harvested the wood and mined the graphite to those who saved to invest in the pencil factory—cooperate to create this useful everyday object. Here's Milton Friedman describing how, in the free market, individuals cooperate for the greater good (in this case, to produce a pencil) in a way government could never mandate or even plan:

> None of the thousands of persons involved in producing the pencil performed his task because he wanted a pencil. Some among them never saw a pencil and would not know what it is for. Each saw his work as a way to get the goods and services he wanted—goods and services we produced in order to get the pencil we wanted. Every time we go to the store and buy a pencil, we are exchanging a little bit of our services for the infinitesimal amount of services that each of the thousands contributed toward producing the pencil.
>
> It is even more astounding that the pencil was ever produced. No one sitting in a central office

gave orders to these thousands of people. No military police enforced the orders that were not given. These people live in many lands, speak different languages, practice different religions, may even hate one another—yet none of these differences prevented them from cooperating to produce a pencil.

We've all heard of Adam Smith's "invisible hand," which directs a free economy through thousands upon thousands of individual decisions that almost magically add up to create large systems of social cooperation—and social good. Read's story of how a pencil is made is a perfect way to illustrate this pretty abstract concept. And it's a timely reminder of a critical part of the greatness of America: our economic freedom. You would think that after all the failed, blood-soaked attempts to create other, supposedly less "greedy" economic systems in the last century, the accusation that capitalism is evil would be on the ash heap of history along with those tyrannical regimes. Alas, some things never change, and capitalism seems to need defending these days more than ever.

Four

RAISING (SMALL-*r*) REPUBLICANS

Like lots of moms, I have a tendency to mark time in terms of my family. When was I last in Ohio? That was with Piper, when she lost a top tooth. September 2008? That was when Track deployed for Iraq, and I experienced my first month on the campaign trail with John McCain. And the early spring of that same year? That was when we were working in Juneau on the Alaska natural gas pipeline, and our precious son Trig came into our lives.

My family is my true north. Todd; Track; Bristol;

Willow; Piper; Trig; my grandson, Tripp; my mom and dad; Todd's folks—they are what keep me sane, grounded, and focused on the future. They make all the bad stuff worth it and all the good stuff twice as good. I can't imagine what I would do without them.

For me, the rule is put your family first, because our families are the most loyal friends and greatest blessings we have in life. I was blessed to grow up in a great family that was—and is—a tight-knit group. I've always known they have my back, that if I tried and failed, they'd be there to pick me up, and if I tried and succeeded, well, they'd be there to keep me down to earth.

When I was a kid, my family's idea of a great vacation was to hike the Chilkoot Trail, the rugged thirty-three-mile path between southeast Alaska and British Columbia that the pioneers used to travel to seek their fortune back when we were just a territory. My parents wanted us to sense the history and pioneering work ethic in this part of America's Last Frontier. We hiked the rugged, rocky terrain to see that history and to experience the rustic rain forest beauty. A sheep hunt nearby would be incorporated into the Southeast Alaska vacation, too.

It was on these trips that I learned about the unique mixture of sacrifice and reward that is family. We were too small to carry our week's worth of outdoor gear and food on our own backs, so Dad did it all. He so wanted us to concentrate on what surrounded us that he carried literal and figurative burdens on his back, sacrificing his own comfort for his kids'. It occurred to me, while atop the peak of the famous Chilkoot Pass, looking down at the jagged black rocks we'd still need to conquer to get to the other side, that Dad had five sleeping bags on his back, both tents, most of the food, and the emergency gear, all packed in, on, under, and through his backpack. Mom carried most of the rest. We kids had our own backpacks with, no doubt, minimal weight to slow us down. Dad didn't say a word about carrying the extra weight. All week he and Mom exercised this cumbersome commitment to our comfort, while sacrificing their own. So now, even in little things—such as packing the diaper bag that seems to have been banging against my thigh for more than twenty straight years now without many breaks, or lugging around bulky car seats while exchanging them from one rig to another, or packing the 4,000th peanut butter sandwich in the 4,000th brown paper lunch sack—it helps to picture Mom and Dad with their bulging backpacks, mile after mile on the Chilkoot, carrying a heavy load for their family.

Self-described feminists talk a lot about how family

and children hold women back and limit their professional choices. Betty Friedan memorably called the family a "comfortable concentration camp." And of course there was the famous rallying cry "A woman without a man is like a fish without a bicycle."

But in my case, precisely the opposite is true. First of all, family isn't just whom you're born to. Family is whom you choose. And I lucked out when I met Todd Palin. He has been a partner to me in every conceivable way—in life, in love, and in doing battle with the *New York Times*. He is a wonderful father, a wise adviser, and the love of my life. Yes, I was fortunate to have met Todd. If you want to get anything done in this life, it's helpful to have a First Dude.

Secondly, far from holding me back, my family is my main motivation. It's the source of my energy as well as my optimism about America. During the vice-presidential campaign, people would ask me how I could expect to balance it all if we won the White House. I thought, *They really don't get it. I don't balance anything. We do it together.* And if we'd won, we would have done the White House like we do everything else: as a team. And, by the way, Ms. Reporter, I assume you're asking all male candidates this same question.

Having a family gives you a gift that you might not

recognize at first. It teaches you that the sun doesn't rise and set around you. It forces you to realize something that will take you far in life, if you let it: *It's not about you.* In our house, we pitch in and help each other out. Whether it's work, or school, or sports, or competing in the Iron Dog snow machine race, it's a family goal. If it's important to one of us it's important to all of us. And if it challenges one of us, it gets support from all of us.

As I travel around the country I see that everyone is battling something. Everyone has challenges and trials, and I can only imagine it is the very bored and unfulfilled person who describes herself as challenge-free. In fact, I find it suspicious to encounter someone who can passively consider him- or herself completely secure and comfortable. Not only do I think that's not true, but also I think that not facing our challenges limits us. There's no inspiration, energy, or ambition to grow when your head is in the sand. The Palin family is no different from others. We've had our challenges, but we've tackled them head-on, together, and we've ended up stronger for it.

When my then-seventeen-year-old daughter dropped the bomb on Todd and me with her announcement that her adolescence had been prematurely halted and, in most unfortunate circumstances, she was going to have a baby, our little world stopped spinning momentarily.

Bristol was a "good girl," and this wasn't supposed to happen. She was supposed to be playing basketball, chairing the Junior Prom Committee, and getting good grades while working in the local coffee shop. And she was doing all that, thankfully, so she would be too busy for anything else—or so I deluded myself.

I was in Alaska's capital city, Juneau, during my oldest daughter's junior year of high school. Preoccupied with the enormous job of being governor of the nation's largest state, juggling schedules around Todd's job fifteen hundred miles away in the North Slope oil fields, saluting (and worrying about) our son's decision to enlist as an infantryman in the U.S. Army, and busy with our younger kids while wrapping my arms around the fact that we'd soon be joined by our newest family member, Trig, I assumed that Bristol was making only wise decisions while staying with my sister in Anchorage. I kick myself to this day for my selfish assumption. I made a mistake.

The night our beautiful, perfect, precious grandson, Tripp Easton Mitchell, came into the world was a cold one, as December nights in Alaska typically are. Because the new father wasn't there until the end of Bristol's labor, I helped deliver Tripp. And as I cut the cord between my daughter and her son, I was overwhelmed with warmth and wonder. I wouldn't trade the experience for anything, but at the same time I knew it all should have been happening ten years from then. A contradiction? Perhaps. But Tripp is a dream; he's the most beautiful baby I have ever seen.

It didn't take long after that magical night, however, for both new parents to realize how much work—and how little fun—teenage parenting is. But my strong, beautiful Bristol reacted in a way that made me proud. She went to college. And worked full time. And took care of a needy, colicky baby through many, many sleepless nights, doctor's appointments, and lonely, cold car rides to and from babysitters. She worked as hard as any young single mother could possibly work.

Of course we all had to bite our tongues—more than once—as Tripp's father went on a media tour through Hollywood and New York, spreading untruths and exaggerated rhetoric. It was disgusting to watch as his fifteen minutes of fame were exploited by supposed adults taking advantage of a lost kid. But we knew him well enough to see how confused he was during that time, and our hearts broke for him and the price he would pay.

Along with our sorrow, of course, was some justifiable anger as well. The lies told about our family on national television were outrageous. It was excruciating for Track to read ugly things about his sisters, parents, and baby brother while he was in a war zone unable to do anything about it. There he was, half a world away, protecting everyone's freedom of speech and securing America's freedom of the press, while that freedom was being abused to perpetrate lies about his family. At this time I was actually thankful he was in Iraq. If he had been closer to home he would have wanted to clobber his former hockey teammate.

It was disheartening, too, for our young teen Willow to witness what her sister was going through. It broke our hearts to watch some of Piper's innocence erode away. And I confess that I felt embarrassment, too. We were a "normal" family; this wasn't supposed to happen to us. I hoped—and prayed—that my family would come through this challenge intact. There were times when I wasn't sure; when it was everything Todd and I could do not to lash out at the forces threatening our family. More than once, I thought, *How could this be worth it? Let's just go back to Wasilla and stop feeding the media beast. Let's give ourselves and our family a break.*

And then I came across something written by an American who knew a little something about adversity: Helen Keller. She wrote, "Character cannot be developed in ease and quiet. Only through experience of trial and suffering can the soul be strengthened, ambition inspired, and success achieved."

If I didn't know before what she meant, I know now. The past couple of years have truly revealed character. We've all made mistakes. Tripp's father went through a time of apologizing for his statements, and Bristol, with her characteristic generosity of heart, accepted that assumed-sincere apology. It's been two years full of struggling to atone, trying to be patient, remembering to love each other, and watching in wonder as little Tripp grows up. I'm not saying I'd want to do absolutely everything again, but in the end, what Helen Keller said was right: we've emerged a stronger, more united family.

For others who may be going through challenging times, you may feel like I did when a friend thought it helpful to share the Palin dirt she'd read from anonymous bloggers on the Internet one day. She cheerily encouraged me to "hang in there though . . . surely your reward is in heaven!" I looked at her like she was an idiot, grinning through clenched teeth as I assured her we'd definitely "hang in there." But at that particular moment, I thought, *I'd rather God keep the reward that may await in the hereafter. I'd rather have peace on earth for my daughter than an extra ruby in my crown.*

As a matter of fact, if you discount the screaming headlines and lurid magazine covers, ours has been a typical American family story. It may not be because of an unplanned pregnancy that grows on a national stage under a scorching spotlight, but everyone ends up in a foxhole once in a while. It may be a battle for your health, your marriage, your business, your community, or your country, but we all have our battles to fight. And if you're lucky enough to have found a temporary hilltop upon which to avoid the bloody engagement for a bit, then your duty is to assist and defend someone who's still caught up in the war. I'm blessed to have a wonderful family with me on my hilltop. They're my best line of defense as well as my motivation to keep fighting. Otherwise, what's the point?

It's a funny thing about being a parent: having a baby is a life-changing event for the couple going through it, but a pretty ho-hum thing for the rest of the world. Your little miracle is just another screaming infant to just about everyone else. The comic geniuses at *The Onion* captured this paradox hilariously with the faux news article: "Miracle of Birth Occurs for 83 Billionth Time."

HOPE SPRINGS, AR—The holy and sacrosanct miracle of birth, long revered by human civilization as the most mysterious and magical of all phenomena, took place for what experts are estimating "must be at least the 83 billionth time" Tuesday with the successful delivery of eight-pound, four-ounce baby boy Darryl Brandon Severson at Holy Mary Mother Of God Hospital.

The milestone was achieved by Carla Severson, 32, an unemployed cosmetology-school graduate and homemaker, and her husband of 14 years, Dwayne Severson, also 32, a former screen-door factory worker and freelance lawn-care contractor . . .

The miraculous birth is the couple's fifth.

I love that—"the miraculous birth is the couple's fifth." But the truth is, every baby is a miracle, whether he or she is "planned," and whether he or she is "wanted." Every baby isn't easy; quite the opposite is true. And everyone who has a baby isn't necessarily ready to be a parent. But every child is a gift of life that is capable, if we let her, of working miracles on us.

I don't make a practice of quoting myself, but I'm making an exception here because I think this is true of most Americans. In my memoir, *Going Rogue*, I wrote, "On April 20, 1989, my life truly began. I became a mom."

April 20, 1989, was the day I had my first child, Track, and I truly believe my life began that day. It was the day I began to really realize that it's not about me. Sometimes this realization only comes to you later, after parenthood has made you a completely different person than you were when you began. That day, I began the process of becoming a better person. I became more vulnerable, because loving someone makes you vulnerable. But my heart grew; and I became more open than I had ever been before to the pain and the joy of loving another human being so intensely.

In his heartachingly beautiful book about losing a child and finally finding peace in his family, *Somewhere More Holy*, Tony Woodlief recounts a conversation between his wife and his four sons one night at the dinner table. The back-and-forth between the little boys and their wise mother shows how a mom's (and dad's) heart can expand to accommodate all the miracles God gives them:

"Mom," Eli asks Celeste at dinner one evening, "who do you love the best?"

"I love all of you the same."

"But which one the best?" chimes in Isaac.

Celeste laughs. "You are my best Isaac, and Eli is my best Eli, and Caleb is—"

"No," says Eli, the logician in the family. "You can't love us all the same. Who do you love best?"

Perhaps a better husband would intervene at this point in an effort to help his wife extract herself from a jam, but I'm curious to see how she's going to wiggle her way out of this one. I certainly don't know how to explain to them how it's possible to love each of them fiercely, yet for different things. I don't know what Celeste is about to say, but I hope she can explain it to me, too.

"My heart," she tells them, "is a house filled with rooms. And each of you has a room all to himself."

Each boy smiles, perhaps considering what his room in Mom's heart must look like. Maybe they imagine rooms full of toys, a comfy bed, all their stuffed animals. What a little boy can't know, until he has children of his own, is that his room cradles every giggle, every sigh, every squawk, all those skinned knees and scuffed shoes, each dream carelessly or cautiously shared, all the hopes we have for them, every prayer we've whispered over them in their sleep. The rooms of our hearts are full with everything that is them, and when we think back to the days before we had them, we realize how much smaller our hearts were back then.

For Tony Woodlief, home is a holy place, a place "that makes us better than we could ever be alone. . . . It is in our homes where we . . . make children and try to raise them, where—if we are blessed—we one day are allowed to die. If God is not in such a place, in the muck of our daily existence, in our beginnings and endings, then he is nowhere."

Tony is touching on something very profound. Having a family—having a home—is at the same time ordinary and sacred; it's as messy as dirty diapers and as sanctified as holy water. And it's by slogging through all the mundane things of family life—the spilled grape juice, the adolescent rages, and the interminable games of hide and seek—that we truly give of ourselves and become the people we were meant to be.

More important, it turns out that it's the *quantity* of time we spend—not the *quality*—that is best for our kids. Busy parents like to comfort themselves that they can make up for not being there by occasional bursts of special activities. But you can't just plan on being a good parent; you have to earn it. Journalist and *Weekly Standard* editor Fred Barnes put it well:

Forget quality time. You can't plan magic moments or bonding with epiphanies in dealing with kids. What matters is quantity time. Judging from my own experience—four kids—children crave prolonged attention, preferably undivided. They want whole days and nights of it. . . . Woody Allen may be a lousy father, but his rule for life applies to being a father. Yep, 90 percent of fatherhood is just showing up.

For those of us lucky enough to be parents, there is no greater proof of the existence of God than to look into the face of your new baby. You are filled with the overwhelming sense that you couldn't have created this beautiful, perfect thing. Something more powerful and more loving is at work here. This child is proof of His power and His love.

In the end, this is the greatest gift of family: putting the big things, and the little things, into their proper perspective. Family makes us understand that the greatest things in life aren't our doing, that they're not tidy or predictable. It humbles us in this understanding at the same time that it astounds us with a love that makes all the messiness and unpredictability only add to the exciting challenge that is family.

I remember a brilliant pro-life educational campaign from the 1990s that made this point very well. It was a commercial that showed smiling, laughing children, with a voice-over that said, "All these children have something in common. All of them were unplanned pregnancies that could have ended in abortion. But their parents toughed it out and discovered that sometimes the best things in life aren't planned." And it ended with the simple message: "Life: What a beautiful choice." There was no call for legal action and no guilt ascribed—just a simple message affirming life and reminding Americans that being open to life and family is beautiful; that it creates something beautiful that can enrich their lives in ways they never dreamed possible.

I think that's one of the tragedies with our leadership in Washington today. It claims to be about progress and making our lives better. But by asserting more and more government control over us, it actually disrespects our humanity. So many voices in our politics today are trying to convince us that, with enough of the taxpayers' money and enough bureaucratic control, we can correct all that is wrong with humanity and, as the president so immodestly put it, stop "the rise of the oceans and heal the planet." But this is politics posing as religion. And the great thing about family is that it has a way of cutting through all this. It's the love we have for a child that has the potential, more than anything else, to expose all the utopian promises of men for the lies that they are.

I thought about this when I heard President Obama mention what his eleven-year-old daughter, Malia, said to him one morning during the Gulf oil spill. He was shaving when Malia popped her head into the room and asked innocently, "Did you plug the hole yet, Daddy?"

Who among us hasn't had the experience of a simple question from an innocent child bringing our ego crashing back to earth? Of course Malia's daddy hadn't "plugged the hole"—because doing so was beyond his capability, even as the most powerful man in the world. The faith of a daughter in her father's ability to work wonders—from protecting her from things that go bump in the night to fixing a broken bicycle chain—is a part of family life to be cherished and preserved for as long as we possibly can. But as Americans, Malia's sweet question should also remind us that we're not children, and President Obama is not our father. Government can't work wonders—sometimes it can't do anything at all—and it shouldn't (unlike real fathers) even try.

By reminding us that we are fallible and fallen, families show us in concrete, everyday terms that which is not. I picked up the book *Witness* again for the first time in a long time. It is the first-person account of an American, Whittaker Chambers, who was a spy for the Soviet Union in the 1930s. Chambers eventually renounced communism and turned in his fellow spy, high-ranking State Department official Alger Hiss. Hiss sued Chambers for libel, and the trial that ensued captured the world's attention.

The Hiss-Chambers case as told in *Witness* is a genuinely intriguing cold war spy story. But more important to me is the story of redemption in *Witness*, and the role family plays in it. For Chambers, communism was once his religion. *Witness* tells the story of his path away from communism and toward God—and the high price he paid for traveling it. The book opens with a beautiful letter from Chambers to his children. In it, he describes the critical moment he began to break with communism:

I was sitting in our apartment on St. Paul Street in Baltimore. It was shortly before we moved to Alger Hiss's apartment in Washington. My daughter was in her high chair. I was watching her eat. She was the most miraculous thing that had ever happened in my life. I liked to watch her even when she smeared porridge on her face or dropped it meditatively on the floor. My eye came to rest on the delicate convolutions of her ear—those intricate, perfect ears. The thought passed through my mind: "No, those ears were not created by any chance coming together of atoms in nature (the Communist view). They could have been created only by immense design." The thought was involuntary and unwanted. I crowded it out of my mind, but I never wholly forgot it or the occasion. I had to crowd it out of my mind. If I had completed it, I should have had to say: Design presupposes God. I did not then know that, at that moment, the finger of God was first laid upon my forehead.

That's a wonderful way to put it: Our families lay the finger of God on our foreheads. They bring us closer to our Creator, but they also bring us closer to our communities and the wider world. Understanding parenthood brings you out of yourself, not just spiritually but socially as well; it takes you beyond an often isolated, self-focused world and into the wider community. When you're a parent, a stepparent, or any caretaker of a young life, you have an investment in the world—a child—and you want to make sure that the world is a safe, welcoming, and prosperous place for her.

Unlike about the nature of our freedom and what constitutes good government, America's Founders didn't write much about family. You won't find any mention of family or marriage in the Constitution. Part of the reason should be obvious: family simply wasn't on the agenda in Philadelphia in 1787. The Founders had gathered to establish a form of government that would honor the principles of the Declaration of Independence and ensure the preservation of the union, not delve into the private lives of Americans.

But from what I've read, family life at the time of the founding was a lot like family life for Americans today: full of challenges, sure, but also full of simple pleasures. I came across a wonderful book written just a few years after independence, in 1782, by an emigrant Frenchman turned American farmer with the impressive name of J. Hector St. John de Crèvecoeur. The book is a series of letters from Crèvecoeur to a friend in England attempting to answer the question "What, then, is the American, this new man?" In addition to amazing insights about the new world and its inhabitants, Crèvecoeur's letters are full of truths that all husbands and fathers would recognize, such as the peace and joy that wives (!) and children bring. This passage, in particular, spoke to me:

At home my happiness springs from very different objects; the gradual unfolding of my children's reason, the study of their dawning tempers attract all my paternal attention. I have to contrive little punishments for their little faults, small encouragements for their good actions, and a variety of other expedients dictated by various occasions.

What father today—or what mother, for that matter—doesn't recognize the subtle art of guiding and teaching children? The wonderful thing about America is that our Founders didn't set out to intervene in these intimate details of Americans' lives. They understood that this was—and should be—beyond the proper scope of government.

The Founders simply took it for granted that a republic relies on informed and virtuous citizens, and that informed and virtuous citizens are created in turn by strong families. Some think this view is no longer relevant today because the men who held it were old white guys who don't represent the diverse country America has become. And it's true that the famous Founders were white and male. One important exception to the largely male, largely white perspective of the Founders was that of Abigail Adams, the wife of America's second president, John Adams. The wonderful letters between Abigail and John, I've found, offer the best insights into the role the family was meant to play in the new republic.

During the 2008 vice-presidential campaign I was sent a book of these letters. And the more I read about Abigail, the more she became a hero to me. She had a brilliant, insightful mind that, like so many female minds, played a powerful if indirect role in shaping America. She endured long separations from John, which forced her to run the family farm and raise four children alone. But busy as she was, she took the time to encourage John, who was off at the Constitutional Convention in Philadelphia, to promote independence for women. "Remember the ladies," she admonished her husband:

> Patriotism in the female Sex is the most disinterested of all virtues. Excluded from honours and from offices, we cannot attach ourselves to the State or Government from having held a place of Eminence. . . . Deprived of a voice in Legislation, obliged to submit to those Laws which are imposed upon us, is it not sufficient to make us indifferent to the publick Welfare? Yet all history and every age exhibit Instances of patriotic virtue in the female sex; which considering our situation equal the most Heroick of yours.

You go, girl. Abigail and John also exchanged many letters about the upbringing of their children. These letters echo in the most intimate way the Founders' understanding of the importance of the family in America. "The foundation of national morality must be laid in private families," John Adams wrote. This was critical because, as he later wrote to a friend, "public virtue is the only Foundation of Republics. There must be a positive Passion for the public good, the public interest, Honor, Power and Glory, established in the Mind of the People, or there can be no Republican Government, nor any real Liberty." John and Abigail Adams agreed that raising small-r republicans meant raising good and decent children. As John wrote to Abigail:

> It should be your care, therefore, and mine, to elevate the minds of our children and exalt their courage; to accelerate and animate their industry and activity; to excite in them an habitual contempt of meanness, abhorrence of injustice and inhumanity, and an ambition to excel in every capacity, faculty, and virtue. If we suffer their minds to grovel and creep in infancy, they will grovel all their lives.

The Adamses must have heeded their own advice. Their son John Quincy Adams went on to become the sixth president of the United States.

Still, the Adamses' wonderful insights on family life

were the exception for the time. It sounds strange to us today, given how preoccupied we can be with the problems the family faces, that the men who laid the foundation of our republic said so little about the institution of the family. But this fact is itself a tribute to the system of government they created. The Founders took it for granted that strong families instilled in children the habits and disciplines necessary for those children to govern themselves in adulthood. Being a part of a family teaches us to trust and respect others, to put their needs before our own, and to avoid shortsighted decisions by planning for the future.

What the Founders focused their energy on, then, wasn't a government that sought to control or shape families, but a government that could capitalize on the virtues of trust and self-restraint that families create—a government that could respect and honor good citizens by allowing them to live and prosper in freedom. The Constitution's relationship to the family, then, was meant to be reciprocal: to depend upon the virtues of family life to make its system of government work, while protecting the freedom of families to create self-governing citizens.

One of the nation's foremost experts on the family, Allan Carlson, describes this reciprocal relationship:

The Founders assumed that most American eyes would be turned toward home, which would provide an ordered society within a regime of liberty . . . Defense of this social order, this society of households, lay with the states and the people. The U.S. Constitution presumed a nation of families and ultimately relied on the spirit behind the Bill of Rights—specifically, the Ninth and Tenth Amendments, which reserved the rights of the people and the power of the states—as the primary bulwark against social experimentation.

Our leaders in Washington today have completely abandoned the idea of a government that relies on strong families at the same time that it respects the liberty and rights of these families. When we have government taking over our health care choices and seeking to influence our end-of-life decisions, we have a government that doesn't respect the sanctity and privacy of families. When we have a government that seeks to tax every aspect of our daily lives in the name of building a "green" economy, we have a government that doesn't respect the Tenth Amendment and that rides roughshod over the more responsive level of government, our state governments. When we have a government that is spending away our children's and grandchildren's patrimony, we have a government that no longer regards us as citizens of a republic, but as subjects of an all-powerful nanny state—which is to say, as children of an all-encompassing, all-wise, all-powerful mother. Our federal government was never intended to become this.

Families matter. This was something that our Founders took for granted, but it's a truth we commonsense conservatives are increasingly forced to defend these days. And it's a case we're having to build in our writing and our governing as we go along. After all, the damage done to the American family by widespread divorce and children without fathers is relatively recent in our history. It was the mid-1960s before divorce and single motherhood really began to take off in the United States. And it was another twenty years before the country really began to feel the effects of the decline of the family in rising crime rates, drug abuse, and long-term welfare dependency.

I thought of this as I, along with so many Americans, watched the horrific images of the aftermath of Hurricane Katrina in late August 2005. Here was a failure of government on all levels—local, state, and federal. At a time of their greatest need—a violent and ruthless act of Mother Nature—government failed the citizens of New Orleans at the most basic level.

But Hurricane Katrina revealed something other than government incompetence. It revealed a population of Americans dependent on government and incapacitated by the destruction of the American family. The victims of Hurricane Katrina we saw huddled at the Superdome were overwhelmingly poor and minority. The hurricane set off a national debate—or, more accurately, a spasm of national finger-pointing—about the reasons for their plight. A lot of the usual suspects immediately cried racism, but that knee-jerk reaction overlooked a few relevant and alarming facts. In a nation in which an astonishing 70 percent of African American babies were being born to single women in 2004, fatherlessness among poor African Americans in New Orleans was estimated at between 60 and 80 percent. In New Orleans, as in so many American cities, this lack of fathers translated into high crime rates (New Orleans's murder rate was four times the average for similar-sized cities in the year before Katrina), rampant drug abuse, educational failure, and chronic welfare dependency.

After Katrina there was a lot of shouting that the victims of the hurricane were actually victims of George Bush, racism, or both. I remember when Kanye West declared that "George Bush doesn't care about black people" during a nationally televised concert for the victims. Although the residents of New Orleans were impacted the most, Americans all along the Gulf Coast were victimized by Hurricane Katrina. And yet those in New Orleans seemed to be the most vulnerable. They all had the same federal government and the same president. What was the difference?

In many cases, the difference was strong, intact families—the families our Founders deemed essential to the success of our republic. The problems that would ensue when the American family began to break down could have been foreseen, and were foreseen by some discerning critics—some of whom were liberals. But the Washington elite and a pack of liberal journalists demonized anyone who tried to call attention to the problem. Forty-five years ago, Daniel Patrick Moynihan, then a Johnson administration Labor Department official, issued a famous report warning of the impact on African Americans from the rise of out-of-wedlock births. For daring to declare that "the richest inheritance any child can have is a stable, loving, disciplined family life," Moynihan was savaged by Washington liberals and accused of racism and blaming the victim.

Standing up for the family wasn't fashionable then and it is even less fashionable now. Many of us remember one of the early and epic clashes of the American heartland versus Hollywood over the role of the American family.

It was May 1992, and thirty-eight million Americans watched as a fictional television journalist named Murphy Brown, finding herself over forty, divorced, and pregnant, decided to have the child alone. Without the baby's father. On prime-time television.

The day after Murphy Brown's baby was delivered on television sets across the nation, Vice-President Dan Quayle devoted thirty-eight words in a three-thousand-plus-word speech to criticizing the sit-com. Speaking about moral decay in America, Vice-President Quayle expressed his opinion by saying, "It doesn't help matters when prime-time TV has Murphy Brown—a character who supposedly epitomizes today's intelligent, highly paid professional woman—mocking the importance of fathers by bearing a child alone and calling it just another 'lifestyle choice.'"

It just so happened that 1992 was an election year, and the vice-president's comments unleashed a torrent of criticism from the Clinton campaign and an avalanche of scorn and ridicule from Hollywood. Hillary Clinton, then the wife of the Democratic presidential contender, panned Quayle as typical of "an administration out of touch with America." Quayle was savaged by the media, and he became the butt of countless jokes by late-night comics. He was dismissed as an airhead, a bigot, and—worst of all for Hollywood liberals—a prude.

I remember the Emmy Awards that summer, when Candice Bergen won for her portrayal of Murphy Brown. The show's producer, Diane English, revealed the sit-com's partisan agenda when she said, "As Murphy herself said, 'I couldn't possibly do a worse job raising my kid alone than the Reagans did with theirs.'" Classy.

The *Murphy Brown* debacle effectively ended Quayle's hope of succeeding George H. W. Bush as president. But from the perspective of eighteen years later, his defense of families with fathers looks prophetic. And in fact it was only a few years later that *The Atlantic Monthly* published a controversial cover story titled "Dan Quayle Was Right." What we've learned since— and what Hollywood is still having trouble accepting—is that families matter and fathers do matter. The left wants us to believe that any grouping we choose to call a family is worthy of the name, that it doesn't matter if children are raised by two loving parents or are shipped off to virtual full-time day care, and that divorce has no effect on children's quality of life. But we now know that commonsense objections to these radical ideas are not based on close-minded prejudice. When it comes to raising good citizens, all "lifestyle choices" are *not* equal.

A fellow advocate of supporting and strengthening

American families sent me an op-ed from the *Wall
Street Journal* by political scientist and author James
Q. Wilson. Writing about the time of the tenth anniversary of Quayle's infamous *Murphy Brown* speech,
Wilson commented on the effects of fatherlessness
on children—and the utility of looking backward to
human experience rather than forward to grand "progressive" political theory—when it comes to the family:

> In our prosperous nation, there exist communities
> dominated by gangs, criminality, and drug sales.
> In every big city, a rising murder rate is usually as-
> sociated with struggles between gangs and among
> young men. These neighborhoods are the scene of
> drive-by shootings that often take innocent vic-
> tims . . .
>
> Everyone knows these facts, and many public
> officials struggle to cope by designing new police
> strategies, mounting campaigns to improve educa-
> tion or supply jobs, or supporting church and
> other groups that struggle to cope with the prob-
> lem. But it is far from clear that better policing
> and education, or more jobs, will produce any fun-
> damental changes. Many people have argued,
> rightly, that the core problem is the weakness of
> families. Two-parent families do some obvious

things. They provide more people to watch over and care for children, and they supply male role models for young boys. And these are not mere conservative shibboleths. . . .

The evidence that mother-only families contribute to crime is powerful. When two scholars studied data from the *National Longitudinal Study of Youth*, they found that, after holding income constant, young people in father-absent families were twice as likely to be in jail as were those in two-parent families. And their lives did not improve if their mother had acquired a stepfather. Fill-in dads do not improve matters any more than do fatter government checks.

Family disorganization is more important than either race or income in explaining violent crime. . . . The sociologist Robert Sampson has shown that in poor neighborhoods the rate of violent crime is much more strongly correlated with family disorganization than it is with race. William Galston, once an assistant to President Clinton, put the matter simply. To avoid poverty, do three things: finish high school, marry before having a child, and produce the child after you are twenty years old. Only 8 percent of people who do all three will be poor; of those who fail to do them, 79 percent will be poor.

The central question, then, becomes a search for the reasons that families are weak. In my judgment, they are weak in large measure because of broad, long-lasting cultural changes in Western society, changes that for blacks were made even worse by the legacy of slavery. Westerners have sought personal emancipation, at first from kings and bishops, then from social pressures and customary expectations, and now from familial obligations . . .

Looking backward makes the importance of families obvious. Looking forward makes families look like an outmoded television sketch—*Leave It to Beaver* or *Ozzie and Harriet.* To many Americans who look backward—conservatives, in the main—maintaining the family, albeit one with some changed human dimensions (such as greater freedom for women), is vitally important. To many who look forward, the family is much less important than female emancipation, personal self-expression, and economic careers. Much the same thing could be said about learning, civility, respect, and patriotism. They constitute reasonable and time-tested barriers within which our desire for self-expression can operate.

In this country, looking backward at fundamental human affairs has another great advantage: It reminds many of us of the greatness of our country. And for some people, looking forward is a way of showing how unhappy they are with that country.

What was ridiculed when Dan Quayle said it in 1992 (perhaps because Dan Quayle said it) is now the conventional wisdom. Two-parent families do matter when it comes to raising kids to be happy and productive citizens. Does that mean we turn our backs on girls and women who find themselves pregnant with no man in their lives? Of course not. I would be the last person to advocate that. I know the pain and challenges that accompany your wonderful, smart, "it-could-never-happen-to-her" seventeen-year-old daughter telling you she is pregnant. I stood on the stage of the Republican National Convention in 2008 with the world looking at Bristol's baby bump under a spotlight that unfortunately created opportunity for critics to try to condemn and embarrass her; I know that feeling. We've welcomed Bristol's son Tripp into our lives with open arms. He is beautiful, and things are working out. But Bristol has paid a price—a high price. Her adolescence ended long before it should have. Her days of carefree hanging out with friends, playing sports, and studying leisurely are over—and she's making sure other girls know it. That's why she's out there, speaking up about her experience and telling other young girls, "Don't do what I did."

Bristol has boldly and publicly acknowledged in ads for the Candie's Foundation that abstinence is the only surefire way of preventing pregnancy. And for this, she has been accused of being a hypocrite. But to those critics I say this: Which is the more courageous course for a young, single mother: to sit down and shut up and avoid the critics, or to speak out in a painfully honest way about how tough single parenting is? I'm biased, of course, but given a choice of role models between Bristol and Murphy Brown, I choose Bristol.

As I mentioned, I tend to mark time in terms of my family. In the last couple years, Todd has been busy building his airplane hangar and gaining more miles in his small bush plane so he can upgrade the aircraft to keep up with the size of our family. He built me an office and studio in his shop, so it's a one-stop shop for us.

Track took over our commercial fishing operation this summer upon his return from active duty, and helped document the amazing resources and people in Alaska for The Learning Channel's documentary on the Last Frontier. He is now attending flight school.

Bristol works full time for a doctor in Anchorage and is also a full-time mom. She travels with an aunt or cousin for an occasional speaking engagement and recently moved from Anchorage back to Wasilla so we could help more with Tripp, and she engaged in an uplifting, family-oriented show called *Dancing with the Stars* to challenge herself in a new, fun way.

Willow has been busy traveling with me, practicing for her driver's test, and babysitting the babies. She spent her Sweet Sixteen birthday party putting up fish in Bristol Bay with her great-grandmother. We had five generations together in Dillingham.

Piper is still my sidekick. I love traveling with her, but she's been wanting to stay closer to home these days so she can go to dance camp, basketball camp, and vacation Bible school; be a tutor in math; and conveniently and obsessively ride her bike up and down our newly paved driveway.

Trig has become an adorable toddler who loves to wrestle and be outside or in Todd's shop. He likes the echo chamber that is the airplane hangar. He rides with us on the four-wheelers and jogs with me in the baby jogger. He's most comforted and content when someone's reading him a book; he can sit for hours looking at his books. He spends a few hours a day at the house of my friend, who has ducks and chickens and cows.

My family spent many afternoons hunting ptarmigan on cross-country skis in the hills of Hatcher Pass. Here, after a successful bird hunt in the winter of 1976, I showed our childhood dog, Rufus, the catch. *(Courtesy of Chuck Heath)*

Family vacations always included hiking in Alaska's wilderness. My mom led us along the Chilkoot Trail between Skagway, Alaska, and Canada during one of our treks in the mid-1970s so we could learn about the 1898 gold rush that helped settle the Last Frontier. *(Courtesy of Chuck Heath)*

Taking a break along the gold miners' path on the Chilkoot Trail, my sisters, Molly and Heather, and my brother, Chuck, were fortunate to have Mom and Dad teach us about the pioneering spirit and work ethic that built America. Here Dad's backpack, loaded with our family's week of hiking provisions, represents his desire for us to enjoy our trips and not be overburdened. *(Courtesy of Chuck Heath)*

Family and friends gather at an Anchorage campaign rally on September 13, 2008, soon after I had been named as the Republican vice presidential candidate. On the front row of the riser are Todd; Willow and Trig; Piper; Chuck Heath Jr.; Teko and Kier Heath; and my mom, Sally. Other family members are seated behind them. (© *Shealah Craighead*)

Touring the 9/11 Tribute WTC Visitor Center adjacent to Ground Zero in New York City in 2008 was a life-changing experience for me. The visit to the hallowed ground was shared with me by the center's CEO, Jennifer Adams, and Lee Ielpi, president of the September 11th Families' Association. (© *Shealah Craighead*)

Along the presidential campaign trail my daughters and I were thrilled to attend a most favorite pastime—watching hockey. The Flyers played the Rangers in Philly on October 11, 2008. It was Trig's first professional game. (© *Shealah Craighead*)

Todd and I gain strength when we put our faith in the power of prayer, as we do here, backstage at the Road to Victory rally on November 3, 2008, in Dubuque, Iowa. During the 2008 election, and in my years in public office, and especially upon my return to the governor's office, our prayer times reminded us of what really mattered. (© *Shealah Craighead*)

Sharing a laugh with Todd the day before the 2008 presidential election while onstage at a Road to Victory rally at Marietta College, in Marietta, Ohio. (© *Shealah Craighead*)

Pausing to greet a crowd outside Sam's Club on December 3, 2009, while holding Trig, accompanied by my mom, who was shaking hands. The good people of Fayetteville, Arkansas, were warm and welcoming during our *Going Rogue* book-signing tour! (© *Shealah Craighead*)

My daughter Piper appreciates a good assignment, so here she takes photographs as I sign books on the *Going Rogue* tour in 2009. This stop was an event in Orange Park, Florida, and Piper loved staying busy with the good Southerners she got to meet. *(© Shealah Craighead)*

Piper watches me shake hands with a soldier on November 23, 2009, at Fort Bragg, North Carolina. We had the honor of visiting military communities on our book tour, including here at the post of the Army and Air Force Exchange Service (AAFES). *(© Shealah Craighead)*

Autographing Captain Christina Valentine's patch while at Fort Hood in Texas was humbling. Our men and women in uniform—America's finest—are a source for good in this world, and I'm honored to know many of them. (© Jack Plunkett/AP Photo)

Todd and I greet a soldier at the PX Exchange at Fort Hood, Texas, in 2008. I always proclaim, "If you love your freedom, you'd better thank a vet." (© Bob Daemmrich/ Corbis)

Piper takes time to work on third-grade homework assignments in November 2009 while traveling by bus with my aunt Katie Johnson and me. My family traveled across America that month, and Piper kept up with her Cottonwood Creek classmates via correspondence assignments. It helped to have my brother and my dad, both teachers, pitch in to assist with the curriculum. (© Shealah Craighead)

Piper *(left)* and Willow join me on a carousel for a *People* magazine photo shoot in Bryant Park, New York City, at the start of our *Going Rogue* book tour. *(© Shealah Craighead)*

Two handsome guys, Todd and Trig, take a bottle break in New York City before we hit the trail again together on November 16, 2009. *(© Shealah Craighead)*

Bristol's son, Tripp Easton Mitchell, digs into his first birthday cake in the Palin kitchen. During the party, my friends Juanita Fuller *(right)* and Barb Adams help Bristol with ice cream and treats for the birthday boy's celebration in January 2010. We've always made a pretty big deal out of birthdays—no doubt our family's collective sweet tooth has something to do with that. *(© Shealah Craighead)*

I play with nineteen-month-old Trig while Bristol supports her one-year-old son, Tripp, on his toy elephant during Tripp's birthday party in our Wasilla home. *(© Shealah Craighead)*

A pleasant Alaskan summer afternoon warmed Trig and me while we chatted out on the lawn in July 2010. Trig's an expert communicator with his sign language, and our hearts will leap when he says his first word someday. I'm betting it will be "dog." Photographer Gilles Mingasson/Getty Images)

After an interview near the Statue of Liberty, Glenn Beck and I pose for Fox News on January 13, 2009. Glenn and I share an appreciation for Lady Liberty. America's most famous symbol for freedom-loving immigrants serves as an inspiration to all: America, continue to be exceptional, hard-working, faithful, and free. (© Shealah Craighead)

The Reverend Billy Graham offers me words of wisdom and encouragement on a Sunday afternoon, November 22, 2009. This time of prayer and a shared meal at this prayer warrior's mountainside home in Montreat, North Carolina, is a highlight of my life. Reverend Graham is a giant in this world, and he will surely hear "well done" in the next. His faith has touched and been accepted by millions. (© Shealah Craighead)

Feeling right at home with NASCAR fans at the Daytona 500 on Valentine's Day 2010! After speaking to the motorhead-filled crowd before the flag dropped, I was honored to shake hands with our troops who were there loving this all-American pastime! *(© J Pat Carter/AP Photo)*

During a visit to Walter Reed Army Medical Center in December 2009, I had the privilege of meeting staff members before Todd and I visited wounded warriors. The staff's dedication to healing body and soul is so commendable, and our courageous military makes me proud to be American. *(© Shealah Craighead)*

Tea Party Americans are standing up and speaking out for time-tested truths in America! It's an honor to meet proud, concerned "we've had it up to here" patriots at rallies like this one, where I took the podium on April 14, 2010, on Boston Common, in Massachusetts. Sharing with them a vision for America that's founded on our Constitution has been exhilarating these past couple of years. *(© Brian Snyder/Reuters)*

Todd is my right-hand man and production "crew" as he helps adjust my television earpiece before an interview with Sean Hannity on one of the nation's highest-rated news shows, *Hannity*. Todd built an airplane hangar for his Piper Super Cub and included within it a spot for me to broadcast live around the world. It's usually a two-person show—Todd and me— when we interview from home.

Summertime 2010, catching up on the news in our living room before I head out the door for a run. Piper and her cousin McKinley are wrapping gifts to send to an Alaskan logging camp.

My dad and brother, Chuck Sr. and Chuck Jr., wait for me to cook the eggs early one July 2010 morning on a remote sandbar where we had set up camp the night before. Nearly fifty years in Alaska and our most thrilling entertainment still revolves around the great outdoors. Sport fishing was on that day's agenda in the Talkeetna Mountains. *(© 2010 One Three, Inc. All rights reserved. Photographer Gilles Mingasson/Getty Images)*

I had to adjust a new firearm before a fall hunt in 2010, so I visited the gun range in Chugiak, Alaska, to target practice. *(© 2010 One Three, Inc. All rights reserved. Photographer Gilles Mingasson/Getty Images)*

My dad and I visit with our buddies, the Wallis family, at their locally owned sporting goods store, Chimo Guns. The guys at this Wasilla establishment gave me good advice on firepower before my fall caribou hunt in September 2010. And it worked! I filled half the freezer with wild game a few weeks after this visit. *(© 2010 One Three, Inc. All rights reserved. Photographer Gilles Mingasson/Getty Images)*

I eat, therefore I hunt! In autumn 2010, after two days of hiking the tundra near ANWR (the flat, desolate, uninhabited land that warehouses billions of barrels of American oil—which we should be tapping), I finally got a caribou. Feeding my kids healthy, clean, organic, wild protein that we harvest ourselves is part of being Alaskan. I often explain that the meat we eat is wrapped in fur instead of the cellophane that customers purchase in grocery stores, so it's important that we're managing our fish and wildlife resources for abundance in the Last Frontier. *(© 2010 One Three, Inc. All rights reserved. Photographer Gilles Mingasson/Getty Images)*

Piper and I flew to the Punchbowl Glacier outside Anchorage in July 2010. We spent the day on the snowy mountain with our friends, Iditarod champions Mitch Seavey *(left)*, Martin Buser *(far right)*, and their dog handler. We loved dogsledding in the epic landscape. *(© 2010 One Three, Inc. All rights reserved. Photographer Gilles Mingasson/Getty Images)*

The Restoring Honor rally on the steps of the Lincoln Memorial on the National Mall on August 28, 2010, in Washington, D.C., drew an estimated five hundred thousand people. Glenn Beck headlined the peaceful patriot celebration on the anniversary of Martin Luther King Jr.'s "I Have a Dream" speech. The words King spoke forty-seven years earlier changed the course of civil rights in America for the better. His niece Dr. Alveda King graced us with her presence at our rally that warm Washington day. *(© Shealah Craighead)*

A gorgeous day near Homer, Alaska, in August 2010 let me lead Piper (in orange rain pants) and my nephews, Teko and Kier Heath, along a muddy beach in search of clams that we would dig for dinner. Clam digging is one of the most kid-friendly outdoor activities we have in the 49th State. It's always on our low-tide to-do list, and it should be on everyone's bucket list. *(© 2010 One Three, Inc. All rights reserved. Photographer Gilles Mingasson/ Getty Images)*

A rare moment captured of the Palin crew—we're all together, at home! Near our dock outside our front door in August 2010 are Track, Piper, Willow, Bristol, me and Trig, Tripp, and Todd. It's really hard not to notice God's hand in the creation that is all around us. We're blessed to wake up to this view and breathe in this air. *(© 2010 One Three, Inc. All rights reserved. Photographer Gilles Mingasson/Getty Images)*

Working overtime—sort of. Todd and I had to wait for weather to clear, so we hunkered down in the garage of Talkeetna's Alaska Mountaineering School in July 2010 before leaving for a climbing adventure on Mt. McKinley. We worked the BlackBerrys before our small airplane could take off for the Ruth Glacier, where we'd change into hiking gear and traverse crevasses, ice slides, and rock to get a spectacular view of North America's highest peak, which is in nearby Denali Park.

He's healthy, and a very happy baby, rowdy and wild, just the way we like 'em!

But while my family has been busy growing and developing, America and the American family have been under almost continuous assault. We didn't want it, couldn't afford it, and it made no sense, but Washington passed Obamacare anyway, raising our bills and limiting our freedom of choice in dealing with one of our most precious assets: our families' health.

Breadwinners are out of work or fearful of losing the work they do have. Washington's answer is to tax and borrow and spend our way out of our problems. It hasn't worked, but they just keep proposing big new programs with giant price tags, digging us deeper into debt—and sticking our kids with the bill.

And as all this has happened, I've noticed something: at the same time they are busy downplaying the importance of the traditional family, liberals are busy justifying expanding government in the name of "the children." Invoking "the children" is a lot like introducing race into a conversation: it shuts discussion down. Anything and everything is justified in the name of "the children." It's quite convenient.

What's more, liberals often seek to blur the distinctions between our own and other people's children. I have heard liberals claim that we "have to start thinking and believing that there isn't any such thing as someone else's child." But this is madness. How can we know what it means to care about *any* children until we first fulfill our obligations to our own? To be responsible to "all children" is to be responsible for none; instead, it is to call for the creation of a suffocating state that erases all freedom and human attachment in the name of caring for "the children."

As a person of faith, I truly believe we have an obligation to the children—all children. But as Reverend Bill Banuchi of the Marriage and Family Savers Institute reminds us, we are given this obligation as free human beings, not as subjects ordered by an all-powerful government.

Jesus' teachings called for "healing the sick," caring for the "least of these," caring for widows and orphans, and generally, caring for any disadvantaged persons who need help. This is the Biblical imperative. But there is a fundamental truth that cannot be overlooked without missing the whole point of Christ's message: These instructions were addressed to free people, not to governing bodies. Jesus didn't say, "Be faithful in your payment of taxes to Caesar so that Caesar can care for the sick." He always addressed the people, because it was the responsibility of individuals to act out of genuine care and concern for others, not the responsibility of an impersonal government body.

As parents, we mark time in terms of our families because kids are the best things in our lives. My friend, the radio talk show host Laura Ingraham, has a great line: "What's the most promising ingredient in this messed-up world? A child." Our families embody our hopes and dreams. Our Founders understood that respecting and honoring a family's love is the key to being free. Today the fight for my family's future is the fight for all American families' futures.

Now *there's* a cause "for the children" that I can really support.

Five

THE RISE OF THE MAMA GRIZZLIES

In Alaska, the only thing we take more seriously than a grizzly bear is a mama grizzly with cubs to protect. Some misguided souls—particularly in the Lower 48—are determined to portray these bears as cute and cuddly. We call this "bear propaganda." Grizzly bears—mamas or otherwise—are beautiful, ferocious, serious-as-a-heart-attack creatures. When you come upon one, you don't give her a hug. You tread lightly. Because when the ones she loves are threatened, she rises up.

So it's with only a little bit of overstatement that I

call so many of the new generation of American women leaders—many of whom I've met on the campaign trail and in the towns and cities of America—mama grizzlies. These are tough, serious, formidable women like Michele Bachmann of Minnesota, Nikki Haley of South Carolina, Susana Martinez of New Mexico, and Carly Fiorina of California. These women are at the forefront of a new wave of strong, confident American women who are positively affecting not just the Republican Party, but America itself. They're building businesses, managing charities, leading men and women in government—and, while they're at it, raising families.

Michele Bachmann is a congresswoman from the sixth district of Minnesota, the first Republican woman elected to the House from her state. She's a small-government, low-tax, pro–energy independence phenomenon who's also a small-business owner and a mother of five. Nikki Haley has captured the nation's attention as an Indian American woman who's also a pro-family, commonsense constitutional conservative eager to take back her country. She's a sister, as is Carly Fiorina, a pro-life, fiscal conservative knocking down barriers in blue-state California. Susana Martinez is a veteran district attorney and a Republican who wins elections in a county in which Democrats outnumber Republicans three to one.

Some people are calling the emergence of these successful conservative female leaders a new phenomenon in America—as if we'd just invented smart, capable women who also believe in the Constitution, the sanctity of life, and American exceptionalism. Truth is, mama grizzlies have been with us for a long time. These are the same women who settled the frontier, drove the wagons, ploughed the fields, ran cattle, taught their kids, raised their families—and fought for women's rights. These women are like America itself: strong and self-sufficient. Not bound by what society says they should do and be, but determined to create their own destinies.

No, mama grizzlies aren't a new phenomenon in America. What *is* new is our determination to rise up and take our country back before it's too late. All across this great country, women are standing up and speaking out for commonsense solutions to the problems we face. In other times, most women with small children to take care of and bills to pay—women like South Dakota's Kristi Noem (three kids) or New Hampshire's Kelly Ayotte (a five-year-old and a two-year-old)—may have thought they should leave politics to others. But these days, the stakes are so high—the future we want for our kids and grandkids is so threatened—that we feel we have no choice but to get involved.

That's certainly how I felt when, as a young mother in Wasilla, I got involved in local politics for the first time. All I wanted to do was lend a hand in my community, trying to help solve some day-to-day problems that directly affected my family, friends, and neighbors. Little did I know where that first step would lead me. I suspect the same is true of many of the younger conservative women who are taking their first steps in politics today.

It makes sense that moms would be at the forefront of the great American awakening we're experiencing. Moms can be counted on to fight for their children's future. And when politicians start handing our kids the bill for their cronyism and irresponsibility—when they engage in generational theft—moms rise up. We shouldn't have to work for government; our government should work for us.

When I was tapped for the Republican vice-presidential nomination I got a lot of, quite frankly, sexist criticism for pursuing the White House while I had a family with small children. Some of it came from conservatives who didn't think a woman had any business being on the campaign trail with young children. I'm used to that; I've heard it since I first entered politics two decades ago. But most of it came from liberals who claimed to believe that women should pursue careers outside the home. Because they couldn't very well criticize me for running for vice-president, they resorted to another low form of left-wing criticism: calling me a hypocrite. They said I was being hypocritical about running for office while I had small children because conservatives supposedly had rules about that kind of thing. (This is why, by the way, liberals love to accuse conservatives of being hypocrites. After all, you have to have standards to be accused of violating them!) Problem was, there was nothing in anything I advocated then (or since) that isn't empowering to women and doesn't encourage them to be all they can be.

What the American people are showing they understand is that the rise of the mama grizzlies is a healthy development, not just for women but for our country. It's the women's movement coming full circle, from demanding a seat at the table to sharing control of the table to provide a better future for our kids.

I believe that some in the radical feminist movement of the 1960s and '70s became too heavily invested in the idea of women as powerless. They were preoccupied with themselves and their frustration to the degree that they made victims of themselves. But as columnist and former White House speechwriter Mary Kate Cary explains, mama grizzlies reject the notion of women as victims. They aren't winning votes just because they're women but because they are offering real solutions and a real alternative to the status quo:

> Betty Friedan's 1963 bestseller, *The Feminine Mystique*, opens with these words: "The problem lay buried, unspoken, for many years in the minds of American women. It was a strange stirring, a sense of dissatisfaction, a yearning that women suffered in the middle of the 20th century in the United States. Each suburban wife struggled with it alone. As she made the beds, shopped for groceries, matched slipcover material, ate peanut butter sandwiches with her children, chauffeured Cub Scouts and Brownies, lay beside her husband at night—she was afraid to ask even of herself the silent question— 'Is this all?' "

And so the "problem that has no name," as Friedan put it, was born—and with it, modern feminism. Fast-forward forty-six years to the beginning of the twenty-first century in the United States. There's a new generation of women my age who, while chauffeuring the Cub Scouts and Brownies, have silently watched out-of-control government spending, massive deficits left for our children, bailout after bailout of bankrupt industries, shady deals to win health care votes, and ethical and moral lapses from all types of politicians. Those women have also asked the question "Is this all?"—and not liking the answer, they are running for office.

And voters, also not liking the answer, are voting for them.

For more than 150 years the women's movement in America has been advocating for more women in public office—and they've been right! Women have a unique perspective. Typically, they are less ambitious for superifical power than men and more focused on providing for the needs of others. I think we appreciate, more than some men, the fullness of American life, everything from raising decent kids to protecting our national security. If I do say so myself, most women have the stamina for endless multitasking and the ability to bring about consensus on tough issues. And we're not afraid to work hard and get our hands dirty. We're busy enough to know that time must be spent efficiently; in fact we're too busy to waste time with typical political games and power struggles.

One of my personal heroes is former British prime minister Margaret Thatcher. Her life and career serve as a blueprint for overcoming the odds and challenging the status quo as a woman. She started life as a grocer's daughter in a small English town, living above the store with her sister and parents. From these humble beginnings she went on to Oxford and a seat in Parliament. In the 1970s she was secretary of state for education and science in a conservative government that sold out virtually all of its free market principles. Disgusted, she ran for the Conservative Party leadership in 1975 and became the first woman to lead a Western political party and the first female leader of the opposition in Parliament. From there, all that was left was the prime ministership itself. She served as British prime minister for more than eleven years, from 1979 to 1990, the first woman to lead a major Western democracy. In addition to being prime minister, she was a wife and mother.

But it isn't just the series of firsts that Lady Thatcher represents as a woman that draws me to her. She is a truly transformative figure. She became the leader of Great Britain at a time when that country was on the verge of bankruptcy, mired in unemployment and deficits at home, and cowering before the Soviet bear abroad. I remember first hearing Mrs. Thatcher speak when I was in high school. I was amazed. I had rarely heard a political figure—and never a female one—speak with so much conviction and so much moxie. Her message was one that America could use today.

It is sometimes said that because of our past, we, as a people, expect too much and set our sights too high. That is not the way I see it. Rather it seems to me that throughout my life in politics our ambitions have steadily shrunk. Our response to disappointment has not been to lengthen our stride but to shorten the distance to be covered. But with confidence in ourselves and in our future, what a nation we could be!

. . . If spending money like water was the answer to our country's problems, we would have no problems now. If ever a nation has spent, spent, spent and spent again, ours has. Today that dream is over. All of that money has got us nowhere, but it still has to come from somewhere. Those who urge us to relax the squeeze, to spend yet more money indiscriminately in the belief that it will help the unemployed and the small businessman, are not being kind or compassionate or caring. They are not the friends of the unemployed or the small business. They are asking us to do again the very thing that caused the problems in the first place. We have made this point repeatedly.

I am accused of lecturing or preaching about this. I suppose it is a critic's way of saying, "Well, we know it is true, but we have to carp at something." I do not care about that. But I do care about the future of free enterprise, the jobs and exports it provides and the independence it brings to our people. . . . To those waiting with bated breath for that favourite media catchphrase, the "U" turn, I have only one thing to say. "You turn if you want to. *The lady's not for turning.*"

"The lady's not for turning." If it weren't taken already, wouldn't every woman want to make that the title of her memoirs someday? What a lady. What a leader. I cherish Margaret Thatcher's example and will always count her as one of my role models. I am not alone, of course. Ronald Reagan considered Thatcher his closest ally abroad and relied on her advice at many points. And it was Thatcher who famously said to George H. W. Bush during the first Gulf War, "Don't go wobbly now, George." There was a woman to reckon with.

The tragedy of contemporary American feminism is that it's had the example of Margaret Thatcher to put forward as a model for over three decades now, and yet feminists have championed a very different type of female leader. Modern feminism's idea of a "real" woman isn't so much a woman as a liberal. "Real" women must be in favor of government-run health care, of restricting Second Amendment rights, of curtailing free speech in universities and in political campaigns, and other liberal causes. In the name of liberating women, modern feminism has wrapped us in a one-size-fits-all straitjacket of political correctness.

This liberal ideology is so sacrosanct among feminists that they label women who don't agree with them as not "real women." Typical was a remark by a Democratic Tennessee lawmaker complaining that Republican women in the state legislature don't share her liberal views. She snarked, "You have to lift their skirts to find out if they are women."

These critics either need a lesson in anatomy or a guide to contemporary politics. Today's self-proclaimed feminists have (more than once) accused me of not being a "real woman" because I don't share their leftist views. (The same sort of insults are hurled at black conservatives like Clarence Thomas and Thomas Sowell who don't view themselves primarily as victims of racism.) But it's actually the liberal women's groups that have little in common with the majority of American women. Most women love their families and cherish motherhood. But all too often the leaders of the modern feminist movement seem disdainful of traditional family life and the joys and fulfillment we find in motherhood.

Remember Hillary Clinton's famous rant, when her husband was running for president, that she wasn't, in her words, "some little woman standing by my man like Tammy Wynette"? Hillary is someone I like and admire personally in many ways, but she came across then as someone frozen in an attitude of 1960s-era bra-burning militancy. She told us in no uncertain terms that she "could have stayed home and baked cookies and had teas" but preferred to pursue a serious career. *Well, Hillary* (many of us wanted to say at the time), *some of us like to bake cookies. Some of us also think we can do that and still have successful careers. And most of us don't think we have to run down stay-at-home moms in order to make ourselves feel good about our choices.*

The women's groups and mainstream media have greeted the rise of the conservative mama grizzlies in much the same way they treated the vice-presidential campaign in 2008: with disbelief that people so alien to them could win the support of the American people. Back then, left-wing feminists didn't know what to make of an Alaskan chick out on the campaign trail talking about the Second Amendment, kids (the more the merrier!), and America's urgent need for greater security through energy independence.

Today, left-wing feminists and their allies seem to

be similarly perplexed. Commenting on the victories of commonsense conservative women in primaries earlier this year, liberal editor Tina Brown complained, "it almost feels as if all these women winning are kind of a blow to feminism." Another liberal commentator said that the true test of feminism is a belief in abortion rights and government health care. It was a new, "selfish" variety of feminism, she declared, that was coming to the fore with the victory of conservative women candidates.

What kind of feminist is it who declares that a diversity of political opinion among women (but not men!) is somehow "selfish"? And what kind of advocate for women is it who laments the success of female political candidates? The fact is that it's these feminist and media elites who are out of touch with American women. They claim to speak for us all, when in reality they speak for a very narrow liberal fringe. The bad news for them—and the good news for America—is that the country as a whole is waking up to this fraud. So many of the voices that claim to speak for American women simply don't have our best interests at heart. We're coming to realize that the empress isn't wearing any clothes. No single group can speak for all women any more than a single group can speak for all men. To suggest otherwise is no less than old-fashioned sexism.

Not long after commonsense conservative women started winning elections earlier this year, *National Review* columnist Kathryn Lopez put it this way:

Women who are running these days as center-right candidates are not Sarah Palin clones, and they're not anomalies. They've been around, and they're fed up. Many tea-party groups have been started between children's tee-ball games by women who see their country in danger. They see so much of what they have always loved about the United States being underappreciated and trampled on legislatively. And so they do the "mama grizzly" thing and work toward protecting it. But you don't have to be an outdoorswoman from Alaska to appreciate that. There's a maternal gracefulness about it. And it manifests itself in different ways, on different issues, because women, just like men, have different issues and different styles and different thoughts and ideas. . . . The "National Organization for Women" could never actually represent us all, and now we're at a point where that's hard for anyone to deny.

And who, by the way, do you think has been raising all those male candidates for all these years? Conservative men and conservative voters weren't raised by savages. Mom might have had something to do with how they turned out.

It surprises some people to hear that I consider myself a feminist. I believe both women and men have God-given rights that haven't always been honored by our country's politicians. I believe women and men have important differences, but those differences don't include the ability of women to work just as hard as men (if not harder) and to be just as effective as men (if not more so). I also consider myself a grateful beneficiary of the movement for female equality, particularly Title IX, the federal law that mandates equal opportunity for women in high school and college sports. So I proudly call myself a conservative feminist. One question liberal feminists would do well to ask themselves is why most American women today reject the label "feminist."

Maybe it's my upbringing in Alaska that leads me to challenge the feminist stereotypes of what a woman ought to be. I grew up in a place and time where women did the same work as men—but were still allowed to be girls. My sisters and I were expected to work just as hard as the boys. We hauled wood to stoke the stove heating our house, we hunted, we fished, and we played sports. But at the same time, we were taught to be proud of the fact that we were girls. There was a time for dressing up, playing the flute in the band, and doing some traditionally "girl" things—and there was a time for getting into dirt clod fights.

For most American women, the feminist movement actually lost its appeal decades ago. The reason, I think, is that somewhere along the line feminism went from being pro-woman to being effectively anti-woman. I mean "pro-woman" in the sense that it was once pro–women's capabilities, strengths, and judgments. Our foremothers in the women's movement fought hard to gain the acceptance of women's talents and capabilities as equal to men's.

As a matter of fact, the original women's movement fought for women's rights in the same way the Founders advanced the cause of human rights: by affirming that we are all, men and women, endowed by our Creator with unalienable rights. I once had the privilege of visiting Seneca Falls, New York, the hometown of one of the original leaders of the women's rights movement, Elizabeth Cady Stanton. Stanton is one of the authors of what is considered the founding document of the American women's movement: the Declaration of Sentiments. It was written in 1848 following a meeting of women's rights advocates in Seneca Falls. In writing this Declaration of Sentiments, Stanton deliberately echoed the words of the Declaration of Independence:

When, in the course of human events, it becomes necessary for one portion of the family of man to assume among the people of the earth a position different from that which they have hitherto occupied, but one to which the laws of nature and of nature's God entitle them, a decent respect to the opinions of mankind requires that they should declare the causes that impel them to such a course.

Can you imagine a contemporary feminist invoking "the laws of nature and of nature's God"? These courageous women spoke of our God-given rights because they believed they were given equally, by God, to men and women. They didn't believe that men were oppressors, women were victims, and unborn children merely "personal choices." They believed that we were children of God, and, as such, we were all—men, women, our littlest sisters in the womb, everyone—entitled to love and respect.

The original feminists were interested in securing equal rights and opportunity for women in a man's world. But at some point feminism began to be about emphasizing women as victims. Instead of being seen as fully capable of taking care of ourselves, we began to be portrayed as in constant need of protection. In the new feminist vision of America, women are perceived as constant victims of beatings by their husbands, date rape by their boyfriends, and self-induced starvation by society as a whole. The message the founders of the women's movement had worked hard to convey was, to borrow a phrase, "Yes, we can." Suffragists such as Susan B. Anthony argued that all that women needed were the same rights as men and they could succeed on their own as well as men. But at some point the message of the women's movement came to be one that seemed designed to support not independence for women, but dependence . . . on government. In short, the message of feminism became "No, we can't—at least not unless government helps."

And liberal feminists and their allies in the media pulled no punches in trying to convince American women that we are all victims in need of rescue by big government. I remember being astonished back in 1993 to hear about a study released by a liberal women's group claiming to show that Super Bowl Sunday "is the biggest day of the year for violence against women." Forty percent more women, the study reported, would be battered that day. The mainstream media jumped on the finding and spread it widely, without bothering to check if it was accurate. Broadcasting the game that year, NBC pleaded with male viewers to stay calm.

But I remember hearing all this and being very,

very skeptical. Based on my own extensive experience watching games with my dad, Todd, Track, and other men over the years, and what I knew about my friends and other women, the data just didn't sound right. Football driving men to violence against women? And women just passing the cheese dip and taking it? It turned out, of course, that the statistic was unfounded. When one brave journalist from the *Washington Post* bothered to check it, he found out it was completely unsupported—but only after women's groups and their allies in the media had milked the myth for all it was worth.

The "football is dangerous to women" urban legend was so successful for liberal feminists that they're at it again today, but this time their target is the World Cup. Author and feminist Christina Hoff Sommers, who first reported on the Super Bowl hoax, has written about how authorities in Great Britain during the 2010 World Cup issued a press release claiming that "cases of domestic abuse increase by nearly 30 percent on England match days." This, too, was revealed to be a misleading statistic. But, as Sommers points out, these manipulations do more than just serve the big-government agenda of liberal feminists; they serve the anti-woman agendas of tyrannical regimes everywhere:

Horrific and systematic abuses of women occurring in other parts of the world demand our attention. In May, while British officials were preparing for the "expected" explosion of domestic battery from World Cup watchers, the Islamic Republic of Iran was granted a seat on the United Nations Commission on the Status of Women. Human-rights activists protested, pointing out Iran's appalling record of tyranny, cruelty, and injustice to women. Iranian president Mahmoud Ahmadinejad shot back that Iranian women are far better off than women in the West. "What is left of women's dignity in the West?" he asked. "Is there any love and kindness left?" He then declared that in Europe almost 70 percent of housewives are beaten by their husbands.

That was a self-serving lie. British women, with few exceptions, are safe and free. Iranian women are not. But the lurid posters of women's beaten bodies and the bloody T-shirts (one with the legend "Strike Her" emblazoned above a big zero) and the bogus statistics give wings to such lies. How that helps women cope with real abuse in Britain, the United States, or anywhere else remains a mystery.

Maybe it's because I'm from Alaska (state motto: The Last Frontier), but I have great reverence for the women of the American frontier. We forget how much the frontier is a part of our national character, even today. In my own childhood we grew vegetables out back, warmed our house with the wood we chopped, and hunted much of what we ate. Alaska breeds a kind of self-reliance that has gone out of style in much of the rest of the country. But the spirit of the frontier still lives in American hearts.

All of us know what this means. Whether you read the wonderful "Little House" books of Laura Ingalls Wilder, as I did as a kid, or watched *Little House on the Prairie* on television, or Hollywood epics such as *How the West Was Won*, you got a glimpse of the men and women who led the movement westward, and how they shaped the American character. The historian Frederick Jackson Turner believed that the frontier was the most important factor in shaping the American character and making ours an exceptional nation. In fact, as Turner wrote, the experience of the frontier produced a "new product that is American"; one that was different from Europe—freer, more democratic, and less focused on class differences. Even today, we tend to move around and change jobs and careers more frequently than people in any other country. It's in our DNA. It's a birthright shared by all Americans.

The frontier also produced a different kind of woman. Indeed, it is a largely overlooked fact of American history that it was on the western frontier that women first won the right to vote. In 1869, more than sixty years before the Twentieth Amendment gave all American women the right to vote, the territory of Wyoming extended the franchise to women. Motivated by both the need to attract marriageable women and the sheer force of the frontier women who worked, hunted, and pioneered alongside frontier men, other western states were the first to follow suit. This trend even reached the distant North. When the twenty-three men of the very first Alaskan territorial legislature convened in Juneau in 1913 (some arriving by dogsled), the first thing they did was give Alaskan women the vote.

The advance of women's rights on the American frontier was the result of the hard work of many amazing women who have virtually been written out of modern histories of the women's movement. Why? There are many, many stories of the grit and determination of these original suffragettes. Sometimes they had what today would be described as politically incorrect views; most times they wore sensible shoes. At all times they were as rugged and independent as the men they lived and worked beside—as rugged and independent as America itself. They could shoot a gun and push a plow and raise a family—all at the same time. Our frontier foremothers loved this country and made sacrifices to carve out a living. They literally went where no women had gone before!

Virtually whitewashed out of the history of the women's movement are women like Caroline Nichols Churchill, a wife and mother who was widowed before she was fifty. In 1879 she founded the first women's rights newspaper in Denver, called the *Colorado Antelope*, which was later renamed the *Queen Bee*. When the citizens of Colorado voted to give women the vote in 1893, it was Churchill who declared, "This shall be the land for women!" So why have feminist historians overlooked her? Perhaps because, in addition to being pro–women's rights, she was pro–gun rights, seriously pro–gun rights.

Caroline Nichols Churchill was jolted from a sound sleep by a hammering on the door of her Georgetown, Colorado, boarding room.

"I paid for that room!" a man bellowed from the hallway. "You've got to get out of it."

It was two in the morning and Caroline was exhausted after a long day selling newspaper subscriptions in the mining communities west of

Boulder. But she quickly shook the grogginess from her head.

"You leave that door instantly or you will have a ball put into your carcass, if not more than one," she called back.

"Fire away," sneered the intruder.

Not one to be intimidated, Caroline snatched up her pistol, aimed, and pulled the trigger three times in quick succession. Three slugs tore through the door, but Caroline heard no cries of pain or thud of a body against the floorboards. She figured the man had ducked out of harm's way and slunk quietly downstairs. She waited until morning to complain to the desk clerk about the intrusion, but instead of offering his sympathy, he demanded that she pay for the night's lodging, however restless it might have been.

True to her nature, Caroline made sure she had the last word about the incident. When she got back to her Denver home that summer of 1879, she described the affair in her feisty feminist newspaper *The Antelope*. Six weeks later she learned that the inn had closed because business had plummeted.

"Such is the fate of tyrants," she gloated.

One of the frontier feminists closest to my heart was

the first female member of the Alaska Territorial House of Representatives, the wonderfully named Crystal Brilliant Snow Jenne. Jenne first came to Alaska when she was just three years old, in 1887. Her family was part of a small troupe of actors who wanted to bring some culture to the miners who dominated the territory. When her father caught the gold bug himself, Crystal and her family made a harrowing trip through the infamous Chilkoot Pass en route to the Yukon Territory near the Alaskan border. They survived a surprise blizzard by digging in a snow cave and living there for three days before a rescue party found them.

After spending some time Outside (as Alaskans term the Lower 48), Crystal returned to Juneau in 1914 and, when the youngest of her three children was thirteen, became the first woman to run for the Territorial House of Representatives. She lost her first race, then her second, her third, and her fourth. Finally, in 1940, she was successful. At a time when she could have, with great justification, considered herself a victim of anti-female bias, Jenne regarded herself as anything but. And at a time when she could have appealed to the shared resentment of other women in order to win votes, Jenne appealed to them as citizens, no more and no less. Here's how she described herself to the voters of southeastern Alaska in 1936:

I firmly believe that what is needed in our Legislature today is a real representative of the people whose qualifications are honesty, common sense, knowledge of conditions, aggressiveness, independence, and fearlessness, together with business ability and experience. . . .

On her first day as the lone woman in the Alaska Territorial Legislature, Jenne jotted down some notes to herself, which she entitled "Idle Thoughts of a Woman Legislator, by the Honorable Crystal Snow Jenne, member, 15th session Territorial Legislature":

Dear, dear, I'm the odd one again . . . I vote "no" to spending the Territory's money for nothing.

I am "invited" (with apologies) to remain away from the American Legion dinner for legislators! No offence, I'm sure. The stag oratory will have little or no bearing on legislative matters, I imagine. Far be it from me to cramp the boys' style! I feel justly proud that these men all know I shall neither weep nor faint if they notify me that my presence is unwelcome.

Watch your step, Jenne. Fight for your convictions, but don't be a wind-bag. It gets you just nowhere. With honorable colleagues facts win—and with the other kind, know your opponent and trump the trick.

My hero(ine)!

Judging by the emergence of the mama grizzlies, it's becoming more acceptable to call yourself a pro-career, pro-family, pro-motherhood, and pro-life feminist. But judging from the reaction among liberal feminists, you would think these emerging conservative feminists had stolen their copyright on the word. Feminist icon Gloria Steinem even declared that no woman who believes abortion is wrong can call herself a feminist. A writer in the *Washington Post* hyperventilated that the women of the emerging conservative feminist identity represented by the mama grizzlies "don't support women's rights, [so] how can they paint their movement as pro-woman? Why are they not being laughed out of the room?" The liberal Daily Kos website simply harrumphed: "Republicans have some nerve."

Some nerve, indeed. Modern feminism has for decades equated being pro-abortion with being pro-woman. In the years following *Roe v. Wade*, we were told that the issue was no longer open for debate and that we should just get over it and move on. But Americans, including American women, haven't simply "moved on" and ignored this issue of conscience. According to a

2009 Gallup poll, more Americans consider themselves "pro-life" than "pro-choice" today—including more women. The pro-abortion orthodoxy of liberal feminists has been shattered by the ultrasounds that now allow us to see a human life forming and a heart beating as early as six weeks into a pregnancy. Despite the Supreme Court's 1973 ruling, American women and men haven't been able to get over the stirrings of their consciences or move on from an issue that cuts to the heart of who we are as a people. Affirming the dignity and worth of every innocent human life and defending the defenseless are fundamental American values.

Liberal feminism tells American women that they can't value life and call themselves women. But more and more women are rejecting this cynical message. I came across a remarkable piece on the *Washington Post*'s "On Faith" blog by columnist Colleen Carroll Campbell that revealed the liberal feminist argument for what it is: a false choice. Campbell explained that growing numbers of women today "reject the false dichotomy of abortion-centric feminism that says respect for human dignity is a zero-sum game in which a woman can win only if her unborn child loses."

For many American women, the feminism that once attracted them with its lofty goal of promoting respect for women's dignity has morphed into

something antithetical to that dignity: a movement
that equates a woman's liberation with her license
to kill her unborn child, marginalizes people of
faith if they support even modest restrictions on
abortion, and colludes with a sexist culture eager to
convince a woman in crisis that dealing with her
unplanned pregnancy is her choice and, therefore,
her problem.

Many women are not buying it. They are attracted instead to the message of groups like Feminists for Life, which tells women facing
unplanned pregnancies that they should "refuse to
choose" between having a future and having a
baby. They believe that the best way for a woman
to defend her own dignity is to defend the dignity
of each and every human person, including the
one that grows within her womb. . . . This rising
pro-life sentiment among women has begun to
surface in public opinion polls. A 2007 study from
Overbrook Research tracked the abortion views of
women in Missouri, considered to be a bellwether
state on such issues. Researchers found that the
share of Missouri women identifying themselves
as "strongly pro-life" rose from 28 percent in
1992 to 37 percent in 2006, with the ranks of the
"strongly pro-choice" shrinking from about a
third to a quarter of Missouri women. This pro-

life shift was even more pronounced among young women.

Abortion-rights activists have noticed this trend, and it worries them. Recently, *Newsweek* published an article in which NARAL president Nancy Keenan described her fellow abortion-rights crusaders as members of the "postmenopausal militia." She noted with concern that the youthful enthusiasm in the abortion debate seems to be on the pro-life side. Upon seeing the swarms of hundreds of thousands of participants at this year's March for Life in Washington, D.C., many of them motivated equally by religious faith and concern for human rights, Keenan said: "I just thought, my gosh, they are so young. There are so many of them, and they are so young."

Indeed, they are. They are young, their ranks are growing, and the girls and women among them are not buying yesterday's orthodoxy about the inextricable link between abortion and women's liberation. No matter how many times the feminist establishment tells them to sit down and shut up, they show no signs of doing so. Let the debate over the true meaning of feminism begin.

Together, the pro-woman, pro-life sisterhood is telling the young women of America that they are capable of handling an unintended pregnancy and still pursue a career and an education. Strangely, many feminists seem to want to tell these young women that they're *not* capable, that you *can't* give your child life and still pursue your dreams. Their message is: "Women, you are not strong enough or smart enough to do both. You are not capable."

The *new* feminism is telling women they are capable and strong. And if keeping a child isn't possible, adoption is a beautiful choice. It's about empowering women to make *real choices*, not forcing them to accept false ones. It's about compassion and letting these scared young women know that there will be some help there for them to raise their children in those less-than-ideal circumstances.

I believe this so strongly because I've been there. I never planned on being the mother of a son with special needs. I thought, *God will never give me something I can't handle.* And when I found out that my baby would be born with Down syndrome, I thought immediately, *Hey, God, remember you promised you wouldn't give me something I couldn't handle? Well, I don't think I can handle this.* This wasn't part of my life's plan, and I was scared.

I didn't know if my heart was ready. I didn't know if I was patient and nurturing enough. My sister Heather has a child with autism, and I always thought, *See, God knows what he's doing. He gave Heather an autistic child because she's the more nurturing one. She can handle it.*

But when Trig was born I understood that God *did* know what he was doing! What at first seemed like an overwhelming challenge has turned into our greatest blessing. All the time, it seems that God was whispering in my ear and saying, *Are you going to trust me? Are you going to walk the walk or just talk the talk?* But when they laid Trig in my arms and he just kind of melted into my chest, he seemed to say to me, *See, Mom, God knows what he's doing. He gave me to you and you to me and this is going to be a wonderful journey.*

I want to help other women who are in the same situation. Women who may be thinking that these are less-than-ideal circumstances to have a child, and maybe I can just make this go away and we'll pretend it never happened. I want to tell them that if you give this life a chance, your life truly will change for the better. Todd and I know that Trig will teach us more than we'll ever be able to teach him. He gives us such awesome perspective on what really matters. Trig has been the best thing that has ever happened to me and the Palin family.

Bristol, too, didn't expect to be pregnant at seventeen, but I'm proud that she chose life. She knew it wouldn't be easy, and it hasn't been. She now sees that what seemed like one of life's greatest challenges is now her precious baby. Not an easy road, but the right road.

I am and always have been unapologetically pro-life. What Bristol and I both went through hasn't changed my pro-life view, but it has changed my perspective. I understand much better why a woman might be tempted to take what seems like the easy way out and change the circumstances. I understand what goes through her mind, even if for a brief moment, a split second, because I've been there. What my family has experienced in the last two years has reaffirmed and strengthened my support for life at every stage. Choosing life may not be the easiest path, but it's always the right path. I've had that confirmation. The timing or the circumstances may not be perfect, but God sees a way when we cannot, and he does not make mistakes. Bristol and I both put our faith in that belief and we're learning together that what can seem like life's greatest challenge can turn out to be life's greatest blessing.

What is hardest to take about liberals calling the emerging conservative feminist identity anti-feminist or even anti-woman is that this new crop of female leaders represents a return to what the women's movement originally was. The women's movement used to be about honoring for women the same God-given rights that our country honored for men. It used to be about dignity and hope. It used to be about respecting women by respecting their choices—whether it is to be a nuclear engineer or a stay-at-home mom—not denigrating them when they aren't sufficiently like men. And it used to be about respecting women's unique role in creating and sustaining life.

Founders of the American women's movement such as Susan B. Anthony and Elizabeth Cady Stanton did not believe abortion was good for women. Quite the contrary, they saw the rights of the unborn child as fundamentally linked to the rights of women. Stanton, who had seven children herself, once wrote to a friend, "When we consider that women are treated as property, it is degrading to women that we should treat our children as property to be disposed of as we see fit."

Susan B. Anthony saw the fight for the rights of the unborn as part of the broader fight for women's rights. She wrote to fellow suffragist Frances Willard in 1889, "Sweeter even than to have had the joy of children of my own has it been for me to help bring about a better state of things for mothers generally, so that their unborn little ones could not be willed away from them." And Alice Paul, the author of the original Equal Rights Amendment in 1923, said, "Abortion is the ultimate exploitation of women."

One great exception to the culture of life promoted by early feminists, I've learned, was Margaret Sanger, an early crusader for the use of contraception and the founder of the organization that became Planned Parenthood. In his book *Liberal Fascism*, Jonah Goldberg describes Sanger as "a liberal saint, a founder of modern feminism, and one of the leading lights of the progressive pantheon." What Sanger's liberal admirers fail to acknowledge, Goldberg writes, is that she was "a thoroughgoing racist" and an advocate of Nazi-style eugenics, culling the human race of its "undesirables." Sanger advocated birth control to keep the "unfit" from reproducing—particularly blacks.

In sharp contrast to Sanger and her present-day admirers, the pro-life movement is strongly pro-woman, and pro-woman Americans are increasingly pro-life. These women and men of conscience are the rightful heirs to the foremothers who fought for our rights at the turn of the last century. These warrior souls show their dedication not only to women, but to the weakest among us: those with special needs, women without anyone to turn to, and children without a voice. They run the pregnancy resource centers, the counseling hotlines, the foster care facilities, the adoption services, and countless other outreach programs that offer compassionate assistance and friendship to women who are struggling.

Those few atrocious extremists who commit violence in the name of opposing abortion get all the headlines, but the real, unsung heroes are women such as the Sisters of Life, whose members not only pray for the protection of human life but do the hard, selfless work of caring for human life. They help mothers have and raise their children, and they counsel and comfort those who have made decisions they regret.

Another remarkable group of Americans who are not just talking the talk but walking the walk of life are the men and women of the website AbortionChangesYou, a safe, nonjudgmental place for women and men who are troubled after their own abortions or those of someone close to them. It's beyond politics or proselytizing, a place that honors the legacy of feminists such as Elizabeth Cady Stanton and Susan B. Anthony by helping women heal.

Liberal feminists like to accuse women who don't agree with them of trampling on the legacy of the women who fought before us. But it's these women who have twisted and distorted the campaign for women's rights into a campaign for everything from abortion on demand to government-run health care who have distorted the women's movement's legacy. Now they're challenging the right of strong, accomplished women who just happen to believe in the sanctity of life to call themselves "feminists." That's their right, of course, and God bless 'em. But if they thought pit bulls with lipstick were tough, wait until they meet a mama grizzly.

Six

ARE WE REALLY THE ONES WE'VE BEEN WAITING FOR?

Everyone who has reached deep down to find the will to run one more mile or press one more set knows the feeling. You never forget that moment: the moment when you kept going even when you thought you couldn't; the moment when you didn't give up even though every nerve ending in your body was screaming for you to stop. That moment stays with you forever and it changes you. It literally redefines the possible for you. You become more for having experienced it. Maybe you don't go on to win the race, but you have a much more important victory: a victory over self-doubt and self-imposed limitations. A victory for the possible.

I come from a family of runners. Running is something you don't have to be particularly talented or co-ordinated to do—which is why I do it! You just put on your shoes and go. And the road, I've found, holds some important life lessons. It may sound odd, but I've discovered that one of the main sources I can draw on to teach my son Trig to overcome the challenges he faces are the lessons I've gleaned from a life-long love of athletics.

Over the years, I've learned that the real benefit of sports isn't the glory of victory or the glow of physical fitness, although these are great things. The real benefit comes from that moment when you find in yourself the strength to do something you never thought you could. More than most, Trig will encounter challenges in his life. He will need to find that strength. For my entire life, running and playing sports have helped me find it for myself. Now it's helping me help Trig push beyond the limits society will inevitably set for him.

The first of the life lessons I've learned on the road, and that Todd and I will work hard to teach Trig, is to take things one step, and one day, at a time.

Take the moment when you start training for a marathon. You can think only about the first mile. It's impossible to look all the way down the endless road and find the will to finish. You have to pick a point—a fence post, a mailbox, or, in my case, a snowdrift—and stay focused. If you don't, the challenge will feel too big. You'll lose your determination in the face of the sheer magnitude of your ultimate goal.

I learned this the summer Track got his driver's license. I was training for a marathon that year. On lucky days, he drove the route ahead of me, placing water bottles and notes of encouragement at points along the way.

Mile 1: "Run, Mom! Love ya!"

Mile 2: "Don't give up!"

Mile 3: "You're OLD—but you can do it!"

Ah, the love of a sixteen-year-old.

That summer, I ran note to note, water bottle to water bottle. I'd get tired or thirsty and I'd think, *Just make it to the next one.* Track taught me the trick of tackling the big things: Take it one mile, one note, one step at a time.

There's another thing about the road: Most of the time, you're alone. It's just you out there. But it's in those times—when no one's looking, when no one's cheering you on—that your character is revealed. When you think you're at the breaking point—when you think, *I can't run another step. I can't do it*, and there's no one but yourself to turn to for strength—that's when you show what you're made of. That's when you discover the hidden reservoir of strength you can draw upon to endure and finish well. Some call it spirituality. Others call it personal resolve. Whatever you call it, I believe it resides in all of us. And when we need it most, it will be there.

Digging deep is a defining characteristic of people of accomplishment and nations of accomplishment. It's really just the common sense that our parents and grandparents taught us: Nothing worthwhile comes without effort. And big things come with big effort. That's what's made America great. When you read the accounts of the women and men who tamed the western frontier, built our great cities, and ventured north to Alaska, you're struck not just by the almost superhuman effort they expended, but by their rock-solid determination to push boundaries, to reach the better life that awaited them over the next mountain range or with the next mining claim. From our comfortable, safe existences in the wilderness they conquered and the communities they built, these Americans seem more like aliens from another planet than our national forebears. But their grit and their optimism are a part of us; they live on in our restless culture of striving and effort and idealism. They didn't just build a great country, they built a great culture.

Few American leaders captured this spirit of greatness and grit like Teddy Roosevelt. Not only did he love the beauty and the wildlife of the American West, but he exemplified, in his life and his words, that large, ambitious spirit. He delivered one of his most famous speeches in Chicago in 1899, when he was governor of New York. He wanted, in his words, to talk about "what is most American about the American character."

I wish to preach, not the doctrine of ignoble ease, but the doctrine of the strenuous life, the life of toil and effort, of labor and strife; to preach that highest form of success which comes, not to the man who desires mere easy peace, but to the man who does not shrink from danger, from hardship, or from bitter toil, and who out of these wins the splendid ultimate triumph.

A life of slothful ease, a life of that peace which springs merely from lack either of desire or of power to strive after great things, is as little worthy of a nation as of an individual. I ask only that what every self-respecting American demands from himself and from his sons shall be demanded of the American nation as a whole. Who among you would teach your boys that ease, that peace, is to be the first consideration in their eyes—to be the ultimate goal after which they strive? . . . It is hard to fail, but it is worse never to have tried to succeed.

How far our leaders have come in the past 110 years—and not always in a good way. When I was growing up, nothing demonstrated the American ethic of innovation, enterprise, and striving—the "strenuous life"—more than the American space program. I wasn't yet born when John F. Kennedy pledged in 1961 to land a man on the moon within the decade. But I have early memories of when that ambitious goal was accomplished in 1969. Like so many Americans, my family and I watched the moon landing on an old black-and-white TV set. As with Theodore Roosevelt, JFK's ambition to put a man on the moon perfectly captured a nation that feared neither hard work nor failure. "We choose to go to the Moon in this decade and do the other things, not because they are easy," he said, "but because they are hard."

I grew up in an America that strives to achieve noble goals, "not because they are easy . . . but because they are hard." But fast-forward almost fifty years, and our national leaders seem to have lost all of Kennedy's confidence and brio (for the greatness of America, in any case; they don't seem to lack any faith in their own greatness). Instead of announcing ambitious new goals for the space program, we have the head of NASA telling Arab television that his agency's "foremost" goal, according to President Obama's instruction, is "to find a way to reach out to the Muslim world and engage much more with dominantly Muslim nations to help them feel good about their historic contribution to science and math and engineering."

Hearing this new rationale for our space program had us scratching our heads. *What? Holding hands and singing "Kumbaya" with Muslim countries? What does that have to do with our once proud and pioneering space program?* One of my kids heard the NASA change in direction and shook her head. "It's like that *Sesame Street* song, Mom," she said. " 'One of these things is not like the others, one of these things just doesn't belong. Can you guess which thing doesn't go with the others . . . ?' "

How condescending to Muslims. How sad for America. And how unsurprising coming from a man who is himself one of the leading exemplars of the new culture of self-esteem. From "paying any price" and "bearing any burden" to trying to boost other countries' sense of self-worth by downplaying our own—all in less than five decades. Is this really supposed to convince our enemies that they shouldn't attack us and our way of life? Is it really supposed to inspire my kids and other American kids to work hard and dream big?

When I finally reached my goal of running a decent marathon, I made it with only a few seconds to spare. It was hellish and brutal, and I consider it one of my greatest accomplishments, I suppose because it just hurt so bad. But it made me stronger, not just as a runner but as a mom, a leader, a citizen. It strengthened me because I learned more about perseverance, self-discipline, and focus—all things needed to progress in every area of life.

Todd and I know that, however much we try to protect him, Trig will confront real challenges in his life. Hard as it is to believe, some people will make life harder for him. It's at these moments that he will need to find his inner strength—he'll need to know it's there, not because someone told him, but because he's felt it and he's experienced it.

Sometimes I think we try too hard with kids these days to substitute this inner strength with empty praise. Everyone's into building their kids' self-esteem by telling them they're all "winners," assuring them that every scribbled picture is a work of art and every chaotic soccer game is a triumph. I understand the good intentions behind this, but I also worry that we're not giving our kids the chance to discover what they're made of. Kids know the difference between real praise and empty praise. When we don't let them fail, when we tell them every average effort is superlative, we're keeping them from discovering that hidden strength. We may think we're helping them, but really we're holding them back.

In fact, we may be creating a generation of entitled little whiners. I came across an article recently that reported how growing numbers of employers today complain that many young job applicants exhibit all the signs of having been—there's no other word for it—*spoiled*. These young people feel entitled to jobs and salaries they haven't earned. They have unrealistic views of their own capabilities. They don't take criticism well, and they demand lots of attention and guidance from their employers. They "were raised with so much affirmation and positive reinforcement that they come into the workplace needy for more," said one manager. Another workplace manager describes seeing young employees break down in tears after a negative performance review and even quit their jobs. "They like the constant positive reinforcement, but don't always take suggestions for improvement well," he said. And lest you think this is the typical insecurity that comes with youth, the culture of undeserved self-esteem is getting worse. We are experiencing what columnist David Brooks calls "national self-esteem inflation." He points to the result of a study in which American teenagers were asked if they considered themselves an "important person." In 1950, 12 percent said yes. In the 1980s, 80 percent of girls and 77 percent of boys said yes.

As parents, it's natural for us to want to protect our kids from the dog-eat-dog competition of life. But do we really have their best interests at heart when we shield their little egos, finish their science projects, and sell all their Girl Scout cookies for them? One of the things that has made America great, after all, is our work ethic. Americans have never been afraid to work hard, in the belief that even if we don't necessarily see the fruits of our labors, our children will. But the ability to work hard and succeed assumes a lot of things; it requires a lot of life lessons that the family and our culture used to teach. One of the most important is the ability to defer gratification, to be able to wait to enjoy the rewards of your work.

Our basic understanding of self-discipline and our ability to work hard for an often distant reward are formed early, in strong families and communities that don't confuse hard-earned self-esteem with unearned self-regard. For me and my siblings, these lessons began early with the performance of household chores and other duties assigned by our parents. We weren't bribed with an allowance; we simply did as we were expected to do as part of the mutual effort required to keep our little family afloat, such as picking berries, hauling wood, and cleaning up after ourselves. Later on this attitude served me well when I had to earn money for college, and when I worked dirty and demanding jobs on a fishing boat or processing crabs and roe on a slime line.

But above all, it was athletics and competition that taught me the value and rewards of hard work and consistent effort. Like everyone, I have to battle with my own temptations to skip a workout and eat junk food instead. But my caring, athletic family taught me to make short-term decisions for long-term gain. I always, 100 percent of the time, feel better when I make the decision to go for a run versus skipping it. And bagging the fat and carbs I don't need instead of consuming them feels better than the guilt-ridden, sluggish feeling I get when I eat a bunch of crap that slows me down. And I know that the choices I make aren't just affecting me; they are teaching my kids. Once I gave up chocolate for an entire year—from January 1 to January 1—just because I wasn't sure I could do it. I'm a borderline chocoholic, so it was one of those "if I can do it, anyone can do it" things I wanted to do, just so I could show my kids. Sure, it's a petty example, but I believe this feeling of accomplishment is what everyone is created to crave. One of my favorite quotes is from former Notre Dame coach Lou Holtz: "God didn't put us on this earth to be ordinary." Everyone is created to be unique, but not everyone has been blessed with the life tools to get to that "extraordinary" place. To get there we have to have self-discipline and make the right choices. You have to have discipline. No one will do it for you.

Our failure to instill the virtues of hard work and deferred gratification does a disservice to all our kids, but it is the kids from low-income and broken families who often suffer the most. Unlike more privileged young people, they have fewer resources to fall back on when they enter the job market with a shrunken work ethic and an inflated sense of entitlement. Attempts to substitute empty "self-esteem" for the hard virtues of work and accomplishment, however well intentioned, are bound to fail. Just like in the competition of athletics, the competition of business, of the arts, of leadership—of life—doesn't make exceptions for good intentions. Greatness isn't rewarded to individuals who "deserve" it more because they come from more difficult circumstances. Reality is harder and more demanding than that. The greatness of America has come from striving to give everyone an equal chance at reaching the American dream, and then backing up that promise by instilling the virtues of hard work, thrift, and fair play. No one ever promised that everyone would succeed; just that they would have a chance to if they worked hard enough.

Our greatest American success stories are those of the least among us taking advantage of opportunity, working hard, and beating the odds. These stories are not in fashion today, but our popular culture used to be designed to give Americans a reason to aim higher. A movie like *It's a Wonderful Life* taught us that working hard and doing the right thing pays off in the end, if not in material possessions, then in the love of your family and respect of your community.

Contrast that with a more contemporary movie like *American Beauty*, in which a middle-class suburban father "finds himself" by quitting his job, lifting weights, seducing his teenage daughter's friend, and smoking pot. Remember the scene at the dinner table when the father, played by Kevin Spacey, tells his daughter that he's finally awoken from the "coma" of his middle-class American life? "Janie, today I quit my job. And then I told my boss to go f— himself, and then I blackmailed him for almost sixty thousand dollars," he says nonchalantly. "Pass the asparagus." Message: hard work is for suckers and brainwashed, brain-dead drones.

That's a seductive, edgy message for a Hollywood movie, but how does it work in real life? Time and again, real-life American success stories are of people doing the opposite—of working hard instead of dropping out; of taking advantage of opportunities instead of thumbing their noses at them; of beating the odds instead of becoming a statistic.

One of these stories that particularly moves me is that of Booker T. Washington. Born a slave, Washington defied the odds to become one of the greatest men of his time. No one thought to build this self-taught young man's self-esteem. In fact, society had nothing but the lowest expectations of him. But Washington had something that too many of the kids being taught to chant "I am somebody" today do not: a positive attitude toward demanding, physical labor instilled in him by a wise, devoted mother and a few remarkable teachers.

In his autobiography, *Up from Slavery*, Washington tells the story of how he gained entrance to a school established for former slaves a few years after the Emancipation Proclamation. After a harrowing journey from his native West Virginia to the school in Hampton, Virginia—a trip that included being turned away from an inn for whites only and being forced to sleep under a wooden sidewalk in Richmond while he worked to earn money to continue his trip—Washington finally reached the school.

> I presented myself before the head teacher for assignment to a class. Having been so long without proper food, a bath, and change of clothing, I did not, of course, make a very favourable impression upon her, and I could see at once that there were doubts in her mind about the wisdom of admitting me as a student. I felt that I could hardly blame her if she got the idea that I was a worthless loafer or tramp. For some time she did not refuse to admit me, neither did she decide in my favour, and I continued to linger about her, and to impress her in all the ways I could with my worthiness. In the meantime I saw her admitting other students, and that added greatly to my discomfort, for I felt, deep down in my heart, that I could do as well as they, if I could only get a chance to show what was in me.

After some hours had passed, the head teacher said to me: "The adjoining recitation-room needs sweeping. Take the broom and sweep it." It occurred to me at once that here was my chance. Never did I receive an order with more delight. I knew that I could sweep, for Mrs. Ruffner had thoroughly taught me how to do that when I lived with her.

I swept the recitation-room three times. Then I got a dusting-cloth and I dusted it four times. All the woodwork around the walls, every bench, table, and desk, I went over four times with my dusting-cloth. Besides, every piece of furniture had been moved and every closet and corner in the room had been thoroughly cleaned. I had the feeling that in a large measure my future depended upon the impression I made upon the teacher in the cleaning of that room. When I was through, I reported to the head teacher. She was a "Yankee" woman who knew just where to look for dirt. She went into the room and inspected the floor and closets; then she took her handkerchief and rubbed it on the woodwork about the walls, and over the table and benches. When she was unable to find one bit of dirt on the floor, or a particle of dust on any of the furniture, she quietly remarked, "I guess you will do to enter this institution."

I was one of the happiest souls on earth. The sweeping of that room was my college examination, and never did any youth pass an examination for entrance into Harvard or Yale that gave him more genuine satisfaction. I have passed several examinations since then, but I have always felt that this was the best one I ever passed.

What made such a lasting impression on Booker T. Washington wasn't just that hard work was something for him, a former slave, to do to get ahead. It was the example of others he came in contact with. In his book he tells the story of being asked to come back to school early one year to help prepare the building for the return of the students.

During these two weeks I was taught a lesson which I shall never forget. Miss Mackie [the headmistress who had asked him to help out] was a member of one of the oldest and most cultured families of the North, and yet for two weeks she worked by my side cleaning windows, dusting rooms, putting beds in order, and what not. She felt that things would not be in condition for the opening of school unless every window-pane was perfectly clean, and she took the greatest satisfaction in helping to clean them herself. The work

which I have described she did every year that I
was at Hampton.

It was hard for me at this time to understand
how a woman of her education and social standing
could take such delight in performing such service, in order to assist in the elevation of an unfortunate race. Ever since then I have had no patience
with any school for my race in the South which did
not teach its students the dignity of labour.

. . . at Hampton, for the first time, I learned
what education was expected to do for an individual. Before going there I had a good deal of the
then rather prevalent idea among our people that
to secure an education meant to have a good, easy
time, free from all necessity for manual labour. At
Hampton I not only learned that it was not a disgrace to labour, but learned to love labour, not
alone for its financial value, but for labour's own
sake and for the independence and self-reliance
which the ability to do something which the world
wants done brings. At that institution I got my
first taste of what it meant to live a life of unself-
ishness, my first knowledge of the fact that the
happiest individuals are those who do the most to
make others useful and happy.

Washington went on to found the Tuskegee Institute to produce teachers to educate newly freed African Americans in poor, rural communities. In the face of systemic racism and official segregation, Washington had every incentive to, as the producers of *American Beauty* might put it, give the finger to The Man. Instead, he worked to pass on to others in need the virtues that had given him success. He didn't take the easy path; he took the hard path. He *earned* his success and his self-esteem. And that, in the end, made all the difference. This is the lesson our children need: every able-bodied American should be expected to work, and your work ethic gives you wings!

It's very easy to imagine the reaction of one of today's pampered American teenagers at being asked to sweep a floor or do some other menial job. We have promised these young people meaningful, rewarding careers without remembering to teach them that working hard and earning an honest day's pay is, or ought to be, rewarding in itself.

Did you ever wonder where the producers of *American Idol* come up with the seemingly endless supply of people who can't sing but are deluded enough to get up in front of a national television audience and screech out a song anyway? Many of the contestants' ability (or, more accurately, inability) to carry a tune reminds me uncomfortably of me. But they get up and sing anyway and are unaccepting and horrified when the judges' critiques begin. Chalk some of them up as victims of the cult of self-esteem. No one they've encountered in their lives—from their parents to their teachers to their president—wanted them to feel bad by hearing the truth. So they grew up convinced they could become big pop stars like Michael Jackson.

On *American Idol*, of course, these self-esteem-enhanced but talent-deprived performers eventually learn the truth. After they've embarrassed themselves for the benefit of the producers, they are told in no uncertain terms that they, in fact, can't sing, regardless of what they've been told by others. But in the wider world, these kinds of instances of hard-truth-telling are increasingly rare. Instead of eventually confronting the limits of their inflated egos when it comes to paying the rent and putting food on the table, Americans are increasingly being told not to worry about it. Someone else will provide for them. I think a large part of the appeal of *American Idol* is the spectacle of Simon Cowell pouring cold water over the heads of these young people. Cowell can be a little harsh at times, but he upholds the highest standards, and something in us recognizes and responds to that.

Unfortunately, Cowell is almost alone in his willingness to tell hard truths. Instead, a growing chorus of voices is trying to convince our kids that hard work isn't necessary anymore, that they're entitled to a lengthening list of benefits paid for by others, and that they don't have to accept the consequences of their actions when those consequences are bad. These voices seem to think that the purpose of government—the purpose of America—isn't to promise equal opportunity but to produce equal outcomes. If we all just magically had the same number of material possessions, we'd all be happy. And their preferred way to bring about this magical situation is by redistributing income. During the campaign, Obama called it "spreading the wealth." Whatever the term, it means government taking from some and giving to others.

The problem with this plan is that Americans don't think it's . . . well, *American*. To their credit, most Americans don't view their lives in zero-sum terms; they don't see their neighbor's success as their failure. In Europe, politicians have an easier time stirring up class envy to justify redistributing wealth through high taxes. Not so much here. One of the roots of our exceptionalism as a nation (as Alexis de Tocqueville pointed out 150 years ago) is that we are not obsessed with class differences; everyone wants to get to the top. That's the reason we work so hard.

But it's not necessarily the money we're after; it's

the satisfaction of achievement. In his excellent new book *The Battle*, American Enterprise Institute president Arthur Brooks explains how, despite what Washington may think, Americans aren't motivated by the promise of a free lunch. Citing loads of survey data, Brooks argues that what makes Americans happy isn't just having money and status, but *earning* money and status.

> Earned success means the ability to create value honestly—not by winning the lottery, not by inheriting a fortune, not by picking up a welfare check. It doesn't even mean making money itself. Earned success is the creation of value in our lives or in the lives of others. Earned success is the stuff of entrepreneurs who seek explosive value through innovation, hard work, and passion. But it isn't just related to commerce. Earned success is also what parents experience when their children do wonderful things, what social innovators feel when they change lives, and what artists feel when they create something of beauty. People who believe they have earned success—measured in whatever life currency they want—are happy. They are much happier than people who don't believe they've earned their success . . .

If money without earned success does not bring happiness, then redistributing money won't make for a happier America. Knowing as we do that earning success is the key to happiness, rather than simply getting more money, the goal of our political system should be this: to give all Americans the greatest opportunities possible to succeed based on their hard work and merit. And that's exactly what the free enterprise system does— makes earned success possible for the most people. This is the liberty your founders wrote about, the liberty that enables the true pursuit of happiness.

Above all, what Todd and I want for Trig and all our children is happiness. We know that that means they're going to have to work hard, and we're trying to prepare them for lives that will consist of moments of both success and failure—and, more important, well-deserved contentment.

But in this endeavor, we are working against a significant headwind. What happened to the old-fashioned American ethic of hard work and selflessness, of trying to build a better country for your kids than the one you inherited? I think Americans still believe in this, despite all the promises of a free lunch being dangled in front of them by their government.

There is narcissism in our leaders in Washington today. There's a quasi-religious feeling to the message coming from them. They are trying to convince us that not only are they our saviors, but that *we* are our saviors—not hard work, not accomplishment, just "believing in ourselves" and what we can accomplish together through government. As candidate Obama proclaimed on Super Tuesday 2008, "We are the ones we've been waiting for, we are the change that we seek."

I believe in a humbler, less self-involved America. I believe in that simple, commonsense wisdom that has come down to us through the ages: Everything that is worthwhile comes through effort. There is no free lunch. Anybody who tries to tell you otherwise is selling something—usually something paid for by your tax dollars.

In the Middle Ages there were hucksters called alchemists who claimed that they could take worthless metals and combine them to make gold. They were frauds. But America has an alchemy of her own, and it's real: it's when the liberty created by the system of our Founders combines with our work ethic. The result is Bill Gates and Warren Buffett and the most prosperous and generous nation on the face of the earth. We have to preserve in our children not just a reverence for our founding liberty, but a willingness to dig deep and work hard in order to take advantage of that liberty. They can learn these lessons on the playing field, in their classrooms, or around the family dining table, but they need to learn them. Because this is the road not just to their material well-being, but also to their happiness. If I can give Trig anything in return for the many gifts he's given me, it is a country whose citizens still know how to dig deep and whose government still honors their efforts.

Seven

THE INDISPENSABLE SUPPORT OF FREEDOM

One morning, the summer after I turned eleven, I walked out of my summer camp cabin in Big Lake, Alaska, surveyed my surroundings and had a life-changing realization. It's one of the wonderful things about Alaska: When you're there, you're never without inspiration. All you have to do is step outside and look around at the majestic peaks, the midnight sun, the wild waters and wildlife.

I'd done it dozens of times before, but somehow that morning was different. I walked outside, looked out at the Chugach Mountains to one side and Mt. McKinley to the other and it hit me: if God knew what He was doing when He created Alaska, then He certainly had some ideas in mind when He created a speck like me. It was then that I realized that surely God has a purpose for all of us—and He expects a lot from us! From that day forward, I put my life in God's hands. Feeling reborn, I moved forward, finding out that not only will faith get you through tough times, but it will also guide you in the good times.

Relying on a foundation of faith, I've always believed each man is created with a purpose. And it's when we are calm and still that we can sense our true calling. For me, the thing tugging at my heart was a desire to be of service to others—my neighbors, my community, my state, and eventually my country. That desire pointed me in the right direction (some would say the "right" direction). It provided me with what has become my life's work.

For the past twenty years, since I've been in public life, I've thought a lot about how my faith relates to my service. Unlike in Western Europe, where religion is viewed as strictly a private affair, faith is an active and sometimes complicated presence in America.

Religion is at once deeply personal and inescapably public here. We cherish our freedom to worship—or not worship—as we choose. We rightly regard what is conventionally known as our Constitution's "establishment" clause separating church and state as one of the pillars of our democracy. But at the same time we see faith's power to transform lives and organized religion's benefit to society. I know from my time as Alaska's governor, for example, that volunteer clergy in prisons and law enforcement provided an invaluable service. For this benefit and for more personal reasons, we seek leaders and institutions that reflect the morality of our faith, and we rely on faith to make our free and open society function properly.

Does that mean we're a Judeo-Christian nation, solely because most Americans believe in Judeo-Christian tenets? No. But it does mean that the faith of our Founding Fathers shaped our nation in critical ways. They created a country that, in George Washington's words, relies on faith as an "indispensable support." They explicitly disavowed government establishing any *particular* religion, but they unmistakably relied on religion to produce the kinds of citizens that could live successfully in a state of political freedom. And this, I firmly believe, is one of the things that has always made us an exceptional nation.

When I was growing up, John F. Kennedy was a model that many looked back to when it came to religion and public life. It happened before I was born, but I later learned about Kennedy's 1960 campaign for president in which his status as a Roman Catholic subjected him to smears and religious bigotry. It seems incredible today that this was even an issue, but it was highly controversial at the time. Catholicism had long been held in suspicion by the Protestant majority, who feared that a Catholic president would secretly take orders from the Pope. Even in 1960 many people didn't believe that a Catholic could—and many didn't believe a Catholic *should*—be elected president.

JFK gave a famous speech in Houston trying to put the issue to rest. I remember being taught that Kennedy's speech succeeded in the best possible way: it reconciled public service and religion without compromising either. All candidates had to do, the conventional wisdom now dictated, was what Kennedy did. They could hold fast to their religion and not worry about the press or the voters.

But what was it, exactly, that JFK did? As an adult I've revisited Kennedy's famous speech and have discovered that it is actually quite different from the way it is often described. Instead of reconciling his religious identity with his role in public life, Kennedy entirely separated the two. "I believe in an America where the separation of church and state is absolute," he said unequivocally. In the best American tradition, he nobly defended religious tolerance and condemned official governmental preference of any faith over any other. But his language was more defensive than is portrayed today, in tone and content. Instead of telling the country how his faith had enriched him, he dismissed it as a private matter meaningful only to him. And rather than spelling out how faith groups had provided life-changing services and education to millions of Americans, he repeatedly objected to any government assistance to religious schools.

In fairness, Kennedy was speaking at a different time. His repeated assertions that he would heed no "instruction on public policy from the Pope" may very well have been politically necessary in an America that had had only one previous (and unsuccessful) Catholic nominee for president, New York governor Al Smith. Still, his vaunted speech didn't represent a successful reconciliation of faith and public office, but an articulate and unequivocal divorce of the two. It is perhaps not surprising, in light of this fact, that his brother Ted Kennedy would go on to have a long career advocating positions directly at odds with his Catholic faith (which was by all accounts sincere).

In any case, JFK's famous speech did not resolve

the issue—perhaps because it dodged the crucial question—and it is still very much with us today. Thus in the 2008 Republican primary, former Massachusetts governor Mitt Romney's Mormon faith was likewise perceived as an issue by some voters. Claiming that many would be reluctant to pull the lever for a person of his beliefs, some pundits and political advisors urged him to "do a JFK." Just give a speech, they told him, and reassure the voters that your faith will have nothing to do with your presidency. To his credit, Mitt refrained from "doing a JFK." Instead, he gave a thoughtful speech that eloquently and correctly described the role of faith in American public life.

Unlike JFK, who essentially declared religion to be such a private matter that it was irrelevant to the kind of country we are, Romney declared that our religious liberty is "fundamental to America's greatness." And he spoke openly of "how my faith would inform my presidency, if elected."

Like Kennedy, Mitt praised all Americans' freedom to worship as they choose. Like Kennedy, he also declared that "no authority of my church, or of any other church, for that matter, will ever exert influence on presidential decisions." But unlike Kennedy, he spoke out strongly for America's religious heritage, and how it continues to define us as a nation:

America faces a new generation of challenges. Radical violent Islam seeks to destroy us. An emerging China endeavors to surpass our economic leadership. And we are troubled at home by government overspending, overuse of foreign oil, and the breakdown of the family. . . .

There are some who may feel that religion is not a matter to be seriously considered in the context of the weighty threats that face us. If so, they are at odds with the nation's founders, for they, when our nation faced its greatest peril, sought the blessings of the Creator. And further, they discovered the essential connection between the survival of a free land and the protection of religious freedom. In John Adams' words: "We have no government armed with power capable of contending with human passions unbridled by morality and religion . . . Our constitution was made for a moral and religious people."

Freedom requires religion just as religion requires freedom. Freedom opens the windows of the soul so that man can discover his most profound beliefs and commune with God. Freedom and religion endure together, or perish alone.

Mitt went straight back to the words of the Declaration of Independence—that we are all men who "are endowed by their Creator with certain unalienable rights"—to describe a "great moral inheritance" we all share that is not unique to any religion or denomination.

> We believe that every single human being is a child of God—we are all part of the human family. The conviction of the inherent and inalienable worth of every life is still the most revolutionary political proposition ever advanced. John Adams put it that we are "thrown into the world all equal and alike."
>
> The consequence of our common humanity is our responsibility to one another, to our fellow Americans foremost, but also to every child of God. It is an obligation which is fulfilled by Americans every day, here and across the globe, without regard to creed or race or nationality.
>
> Americans acknowledge that liberty is a gift of God, not an indulgence of government. No people in the history of the world have sacrificed as much for liberty.

The difference is striking: where Kennedy seemed to want to run away from religion, Mitt Romney forthrightly embraced it. The contrast is attributable not just to the political distance between the two men, but to the distance our country has come since 1960. We are blessed to live in a land that is reawakening to the gift of our religious heritage. To be sure, there are still lots of voices that reject this gift and regard it as somehow divisive. Where we see tolerance, they see intolerance. Where we see wholesome purpose, they see a sinister agenda. Violence and bigotry committed in the name of religion surely exist in the world. To this extent, the modern critics of religion have a point. We are rightly appalled, for example, at the stoning of adulterers and the domestic abuse of women that still occur in some Muslim societies. Too many also justify their political hatreds and deflect blame for their backwardness by abusing religion. But the critics are wrong to turn these admitted excesses into an indictment of religion per se. For in America, faith has been central to a strikingly different result: the most prosperous, generous, peace-loving, and free nation in history. We fail to acknowledge this profound historical truth at our peril, and that of future generations. For as Mitt correctly said, "Freedom and religion endure together, or perish alone."

"We have no government armed with power capable of contending with human passions unbridled by morality and religion." This stirring quote is taken from a letter

John Adams wrote to the officers of the Massachusetts militia in 1798, at a time when the United States was on the verge of war with France. With antireligious fervor on the rise in Europe, and France still staggering from the bloody horrors of its own revolution, Adams, who had been a leading participant at the Constitutional Convention, reminded the officers that our founding documents were uniquely unsuited for a similar uprising. Instead, they took for granted the existence of abiding habits of decency and civility that were in turn firmly grounded in religious faith:

> . . . we have no government armed with power capable of contending with human passions unbridled by morality and religion. Avarice, ambition, revenge, or gallantry, would break the strongest cords of our Constitution as a whale goes through a net. Our Constitution was made only for a moral and religious people. It is wholly inadequate to the government of any other.

Adams wrote these words more than twenty years after the Declaration and more than ten years after the Constitution was drafted. But even before these great and enduring Charters of Liberty were drawn up, faith played a decisive role in the creation of America.

One of the more overlooked aspects of our history is the significant role that the clergy played in the Revolutionary War. Ministers were usually the most educated people in colonial American towns. And they had a captive audience once a week. Not only did they preach revolution, they also organized militias and fought in the war. For daring to reject the European belief in the "divine right of kings"—the notion that power flows from God to the king or queen, who then decides what rights to grant the people—American loyalists dubbed the black-robed patriot clergy the "Black Regiment."

The Library of Congress's wonderful exhibit on "Religion and the Founding of the American Republic" features one of the more prominent members of this Black Regiment, the Reverend John Peter Gabriel Muhlenberg of Woodstock, Virginia. Muhlenberg was the son of a German immigrant, and is considered the founder, along with his brother Frederick Augustus Muhlenberg, of the Lutheran Church in America. The story goes that Reverend Muhlenberg preached a particularly heated sermon to his congregation one Sunday in January 1776. In his conclusion, he is said to have quoted Ecclesiastes:

> The Bible tells us there is a time for all things, and there is a time to preach and a time to pray—but

the time for me to preach has passed away, and there is a time to fight, and that time has come now. Now is the time to fight!

With that, Muhlenberg threw off his clerical robes to reveal the uniform of a Virginia military officer. Then the good Reverend marched off to join the Continental Army. He served with distinction, commanding a brigade that successfully stormed the British at Yorktown, and eventually rose to the rank of major general. His brother, also a pastor, at first opposed the idea of a man of the cloth serving in the military—until the British army burned down his church! After the war Frederick became a delegate to the Pennsylvania Constitutional Convention and was the first person to sign the Bill of Rights. He later served three terms in Congress and became the first speaker of the U.S. House of Representatives.

Another member of the Black Regiment—a hero of the American founding who may have been overlooked because he combined faith with patriotism—was John Witherspoon, the only member of the clergy to sign the Declaration of Independence. He also signed the Articles of Confederation and took part in ratifying the Constitution. This largely forgotten figure is most known today for being the direct ancestor of the actress

Reese Witherspoon. But at a critical point in American history, he contributed mightily to the fight for independence. Witherspoon was a Presbyterian pastor, an outstanding educator, and a practiced politician. As president of the College of New Jersey (later Princeton University), he mentored a generation of young men who would go on to lead the Revolution and dominate the political life of the young republic, including James Madison and Aaron Burr. He later served in Congress and advised Alexander Hamilton on public finance. He also personified what John Adams meant when he said, "our Constitution was made only for a moral and religious people."

Here is part of a sermon Witherspoon preached on Thanksgiving Day, 1782:

> It is a truth of no little importance to us in our present situation, not only that the manners of a people are of consequence to the stability of every civil society, but that they are of much more consequence to free states, than to those of a different kind. In many of these last, a principle of honour, and the subordination of ranks, with the vigour of despotic authority, supply the place of virtue, by restraining irregularities and producing public order. But in free states, where the body of the

people have the supreme power properly in their own hands, and must be ultimately resorted to on all great matters, if there is a general corruption of manners, there can be nothing but confusion. So true is that, that civil liberty cannot be long preserved without virtue. *A monarchy may subsist for ages, and be better or worse under a good or bad prince, but a republic once equally poised, must either preserve its virtue or lose its liberty.* (emphasis mine)

In other words, tyranny can thrive whether people are good or bad, but preserving freedom takes preserving virtue. You can look, but you would have trouble finding an American from the founding generation who didn't share this belief. This sentiment, so controversial today, was simply taken for granted at the time. The Founders deliberately and self-consciously constructed a government based on the belief that religion was at the root of the personal and public virtues necessary to sustain freedom. And they weren't just being pragmatic. Despite the identification of many with Enlightened Deism, an eighteenth-century belief that strove to reconcile religion with reason, they all had genuine faith and genuinely believed that following its dictates was for the better, both in this life and the next.

In his wonderful book *George Washington's Sacred Fire*, Peter A. Lillback writes about the deeply held faith of our first president and how it left an indelible mark on America. The very first thing Washington did as president was to offer a prayer to God to secure the liberties of the new nation, and his inauguration set two religious precedents that endure to this day. Washington, like all subsequent presidents, put his hand on the Bible as he was sworn in. And he added the words "So help me God" to the presidential oath described in the Constitution. Every president since that time has also ended the oath with "so help me God." (I ad-libbed "so help me God" every time I was sworn in as an elected official, so Washington's addition struck a chord with me.)

Washington's most famous evocation of religion—a point John Adams would repeat when he succeeded him as president—came in his Farewell Address. To understand the impact of Washington's words, it helps to bear in mind that he had, even then, earned the title Father of His Country. He was so admired that some wanted him to be made king. But the American experiment was based on the notion that only a freely elected government was consistent with the revolutionary idea that our natural and political rights ultimately derive from our Creator. In his Farewell Address, Washington reminded Americans that a people made sovereign by their creation in the image of God could not be ruled without their consent. Nor could they long retain their freedom without the morality and good character that are created and supported by religion.

Of all the dispositions and habits which lead to political prosperity, Religion and Morality are indispensable supports. In vain would that man claim the tribute of Patriotism, who should labor to subvert these great Pillars of human happiness, these firmest props of the duties of men and citizens. The mere Politician, equally with the pious man, ought to respect and to cherish them. A volume could not trace all their connections with private and public felicity. Let it simply be asked, Where is the security for property, for reputation, for life, if the sense of religious obligation desert the oaths, which are the instruments of investigation in Courts of Justice? And let us with caution indulge the supposition, that morality can be maintained without religion. Whatever may be conceded to the influence of refined education on minds of peculiar structure, reason and experience both forbid us to expect, that national morality can prevail in exclusion of religious principle.

Washington clearly believed that religious faith is the basis for all the virtues on which republican government depends. The private oaths men swear in the conduct of their business, no less than the public oaths they swear before the courts, are worthless without an underlying conviction in the existence of right and wrong. But Washington goes further, asserting that morality itself cannot be sustained without the support of religious belief. This is not a politically correct notion today. But it remains as true now as it was then.

If you look for it, you will find this sentiment echoed throughout the words of the Founders. Even Thomas Jefferson, widely regarded by contemporary historians as one of the least religious of the Founders, wrote, "The God who gave us life gave us liberty at the same time. The hand of force may destroy, but cannot disjoin them."

I love those words—and there are echoes of them throughout Jefferson's voluminous writings. Calvin Coolidge, in his famous Fourth of July speech, said that Jefferson in fact acknowledged that his "best ideas of democracy" had come to him at church meetings.

One of my favorite stories of early Americans turning to God for guidance comes from 1774, when war with Great Britain was looming. The First Continental Congress convened in Philadelphia as British ships filled Boston Harbor and British troops occupied the city. The feeling that they would soon be engaged in war consumed the delegates. One of them suggested that they pray for guidance. But some of the delegates objected. There were members of various religious denominations present. Who would lead the prayer?

Then Sam Adams rose and ended the disagreement. The idea he expressed on that day in 1774 remains as valid now as it was then. According to a letter John Adams wrote to Abigail describing the scene, Sam stood up and "said he was no Bigot, and could hear a Prayer from a Gentleman of Piety and Virtue, who was at the same Time a Friend to his Country." I love the simple, straightforward rejection of religious bigotry in these words. And like most Americans today, I feel exactly the same way. Despite differences in the denomination you may belong to, if you love both God and country, I'll be happy to pray with you, too. Yes, Sam Adams was correct. So when I recently spotted my nephew, Payton, wearing a t-shirt emblazoned with the logo "I'm thinking Sam Adams, not drinking Sam Adams," I had to grin.

But it wasn't just the words of our Founders—as important as they are—that demonstrate the high value they placed on religious faith. It was their deeds as members of the new government as well.

One of the best compilations of explicitly religious official acts of the Founders that I've come across comes from Supreme Court justice Antonin Scalia. It appears in one of his famous dissents, in a case in which the Supreme Court ruled that the Ten Commandments could not be displayed at the McCreary County Court-house in Whitley City, Kentucky. After mentioning Washington's addition of "so help me God" to the oath of office, Scalia goes on to explain:

The same week that Congress submitted the Establishment Clause as part of the Bill of Rights for ratification by the States, it enacted legislation providing for paid chaplains in the House and Senate. . . . The day after the First Amendment was proposed, the same Congress that had proposed it requested the President to proclaim "a day of public thanksgiving and prayer, to be observed, by acknowledging, with grateful hearts, the many and signal favours of Almighty God." . . . President Washington offered the first Thanksgiving Proclamation shortly thereafter, devoting November 26, 1789, on behalf of the American people "to the service of that great and glorious Being who is the beneficent author of all the good that is, that was, or that will be . . ." thus beginning a tradition of

offering gratitude to God that continues today. . . .
The same Congress also reenacted the Northwest
Territory Ordinance of 1787, 1 Stat. 50, Article III,
of which provided: "Religion, morality, and
knowledge, being necessary to good government
and the happiness of mankind, schools and the
means of education shall forever be encouraged."
. . . And of course the First Amendment itself ac-
cords religion (and no other manner of belief) special constitutional protection.

. . . Nor have the views of our people on this
matter significantly changed. Presidents continue
to conclude the Presidential oath with the words
"so help me God." Our legislatures, state and national, continue to open their sessions with prayer
led by official chaplains. The sessions of this Court
continue to open with the prayer "God save the
United States and this Honorable Court." Invoca-
tion of the Almighty by our public figures, at all
levels of government, remains commonplace. Our
coinage bears the motto "IN GOD WE TRUST."
And our Pledge of Allegiance contains the acknowledgment that we are a Nation "under God."

Justice Scalia makes the point that it is not just in
their diaries or personal letters that the Founders made

the linkage between freedom and religion but also in their official acts and pronouncements as governmental figures. Both as creators and leaders of the new nation, the Founders understood our political freedom as resting on the indispensable support of religious faith. As men of their time, they simply couldn't foresee a future when that wouldn't be the case.

When Alexis de Tocqueville visited America more than thirty years later, he saw the same thing. The America he observed was no longer a nation struggling to be born, but a strong, young republic. He was struck by how firmly Americans and American clergy believed in the separation of church and state, and yet how decisively religion shaped their politics and supported their freedom.

> Religion in America takes no direct part in the government of society, but it must be regarded as the first of their political institutions; for if it does not impart a taste for freedom, it facilitates the use of it. Indeed, it is in this same point of view that the inhabitants of the United States themselves look upon religious belief. I do not know whether all Americans have a sincere faith in their religion—for who can search the human heart?—but I am certain that they hold it to be indispens-

able to the maintenance of republican institutions. This opinion is not peculiar to a class of citizens or to a party, but it belongs to the whole nation and to every rank of society. . . .

Upon my arrival in the United States the religious aspect of the country was the first thing that struck my attention; and the longer I stayed there, the more I perceived the great political consequences resulting from this new state of things. In France I had almost always seen the spirit of religion and the spirit of freedom marching in opposite directions. But in America I found they were intimately united and that they reigned in common over the same country.

What the Founders made explicit in their words and deeds, Tocqueville was able to observe simply by traveling around the country and talking to ordinary citizens. America was—and is—an exceptional place, a place where religion and freedom march in the same direction.

Traveling around the country today, I know I'm not alone in my own reliance on faith. I meet so many Americans who have the sense of unique purpose that comes with belief in a loving and powerful God.

Some see this confession of faith as dangerous. They regard religion itself as inherently divisive. They seem intimidated and frightened somehow, as though any discussion of the religious roots of America's social and constitutional order is somehow manifestly intolerant. This viewpoint seems to assume that acknowledging the importance our Founders placed on religious faith is like saying that only a certain kind of people are welcome in America. In fact, precisely the opposite is true.

The Founding Fathers were serious students of history. They had seen what centuries of state-sponsored religions and sectarian struggle had done to Europe, and they were determined that the same thing not happen here. Men such as Washington, Jefferson, and Madison were well aware of the wars spawned and the tyranny perpetuated when government takes the side of a particular religion rather than protecting the freedom of people to practice (or not practice) all religions.

Reading about the faith roots of America in Matthew Spalding's book *We Still Hold These Truths*, I learned that, from the very beginning, our Founders expressed a profound belief in religious tolerance. Thus at the same time that George Washington was setting aside November 26, 1789, as a day of prayer and Thanksgiving, he was reaching out to different religious faiths to assure them of their equal and protected place under

the new government. (Now we celebrate Thanksgiving
on the fourth Thursday in November, but November
26 is personally significant to me because it is my sister
Molly's birthday. We say a prayer of sincere thanksgiving as we eat cake!) Early in his presidency, Washington
wrote letters to the United Baptists, the Presbyteri-
ans, and others in which he congratulated Americans
on creating a government "which gives to bigotry no
sanction, to persecution no assistance requir[ing] only
that they who live under its protection should demean
themselves as good citizens." And he wrote one more
letter, writes Spalding, to the Hebrew Congregation at
Newport, representatives of "one of the most perse-
cuted religious minorities in all history":

> The Citizens of the United States of America have
> a right to applaud themselves for having given to
> mankind examples of an enlarged and liberal pol-
> icy: a policy worthy of imitation. All possess alike
> liberty of conscience and immunities of citizen-
> ship. It is now no more that toleration is spoken of,
> as if it were the indulgence of one class of people,
> that another enjoyed the exercise of their inherent
> natural rights. For happily the Government of the
> United States, which gives to bigotry no sanction,
> to persecution no assistance requires only that they

who live under its protection should demean themselves as good citizens, in giving it on all occasions their effectual support.

It would be inconsistent with the frankness of my character not to avow that I am pleased with your favorable opinion of my Administration, and fervent wishes for my felicity. May the Children of the Stock of Abraham, who dwell in this land, continue to merit and enjoy the good will of the other Inhabitants; while every one shall sit in safety under his own vine and figtree, and there shall be none to make him afraid. May the father of all mercies scatter light and not darkness in our paths, and make us all in our several vocations useful here, and in his own due time and way everlastingly happy.

Religious intolerance and discrimination on the part of believers and nonbelievers alike would certainly exist in the new republic. But the position of the government was clear. As Spalding explains, in America, having rights was not connected with any particular religious faith or any faith at all. Everyone's religious freedom was protected by the government. All that was asked of individual Americans was that they obey the laws of the land.

This is the kind of exceptionalism that Tocqueville would describe forty years later. Thanks to leaders such as Washington, America became a place where freedom and religion are not at odds but actually support and complement each other. There is no religious test for citizenship. You need not be a good Catholic, a good Pentecostal, or a good Muslim, just a good American. In America, there is no presumption that God is on the side of anyone or anything but freedom. No government of man can legitimately claim to represent the will of God, and no government in America can force its citizens to respect such a claim.

Abraham Lincoln is a wonderful model for Americans trying to navigate contemporary life with tolerance for others while remaining true to their religious faith. On the north wall of the Lincoln Memorial in Washington is inscribed what many believe is Lincoln's greatest speech, his Second Inaugural Address. It is just 703 words long, yet it mentions God 14 times and quotes the Bible twice. But it is no blustering sermon. Lincoln did not presume to know which side God favored in the Civil War. Even though the conflict was still raging and passions were high, he sought to heal the nation, not to judge. And despite his belief that slavery was a great moral wrong, he resisted the temptation to invoke God in support of his cause. Instead, his expression of deep faith in the most difficult circumstances imaginable was a profound statement of tolerance and healing.

Each looked for an easier triumph, and a result less fundamental and astounding. Both read the same Bible, and pray to the same God; and each invokes His aid against the other. It may seem strange that any men should dare ask a just God's assistance in wringing their bread from the sweat of other men's faces; but let us judge not that we will be not judged. The prayers of both could not be answered; that of neither has been answered fully. The Almighty has His own purposes. . . .

With malice toward none; with charity for all; with firmness in the right, as God gives us to see the right, let us strive on to finish the work we are in, to bind up the nation's wounds; to care for him who shall have borne the battle, and for his widow, and his orphan—to do all which may achieve and cherish a just, and a lasting peace, among ourselves, and with all nations.

That morning years ago in Big Lake, I discovered a wonderful truth: like all God's creatures, I have a purpose in the world. We can spend a lifetime trying to find that purpose, and we may come close, but I don't know many who have ultimately found it. Like most people, I join them along the path in searching, and endeavoring to appreciate each step along the way.

I believe my country, too, has a purpose: to be a shining city on a hill, a beacon of liberty and hope for all the peoples of the earth. Our country was created by believing men and women to be a good and virtuous place, a nation capable of producing people fit to exercise the gift of freedom. And for those who fear that people of faith desire to rewrite the Constitution and the laws on the presumed authority of God, let me be clear that I don't believe any of us can claim to know the mind of the Creator who gave us life and liberty. We can only seek His guidance, His protection, and His love.

Eight

I HEAR AMERICA PRAYING

On a remote outcropping in the middle of the 1.6-million-acre Mojave Desert sits a cross. At least, *sometimes* a cross is visible there. For years, it was covered by a plywood box. And when the Supreme Court ordered the box removed earlier this year, vandals quickly ripped the cross down.

The plain white cross has come to be known as the Mojave Cross, and it has stood its vigil since 1934 when the local chapter of the Veterans of Foreign Wars (VFW) put it up to honor the servicemen and -women who lost their lives in World War I. It's in an area so remote that an hour can pass between cars traveling on the road below. And yet, someone, somehow, found the cross so offensive they persuaded a judge to have it covered up.

That someone was former Park Service employee Frank Buono. Because the cross was on federal land, Buono—along with the always helpful ACLU—was able to claim that it violated his right not to have the government establish a religion. How a lonely cross in the middle of the desert amounted to "establishing" a religion is a mystery to me. But it wasn't a mystery to the judges on San Francisco's Ninth Circuit Court of Appeals. The court agreed with Buono and ordered the cross covered up. Even after Congress intervened and transferred the land on which the cross stands from the federal government to the private ownership of the VFW, Buono and the PASA—Perpetually Aggrieved Secularists of America (!)—objected. They took the case all the way to the Supreme Court, which ruled that the cross could stand—and the box had to go. That's when someone took matters into his or her own hands and (in a display of the religious tolerance they hold so dear!) stole the cross.

The Supreme Court's ruling in the Mojave Cross case was a defeat for those who want to purge all religious expression from America's public (and not so public) places. But this victory for religious expression may be a temporary one. The High Court didn't rule on whether the cross violated the Constitution but instead confined itself to whether Congress's transfer of the land to the VFW was proper. The cross can stand for now (that is, if the vandals let it); but Buono and his allies can still challenge its constitutionality in court. Which means that not only the Mojave Cross, but all crosses, Stars of David, and other religious symbols on federal land—including the thousands that dot sacred places such as Arlington National Cemetery—could be declared unconstitutional.

In his book *Rediscovering God in America* (which takes the reader on a walking tour of the many references to God and faith in the nation's capital), Newt Gingrich writes:

> There is no attack on American culture more destructive and more historically dishonest than the secular Left's relentless effort to drive God out of America's public square . . .
>
> For most Americans, the blessings of God have been the basis for our liberty, prosperity and survival as a unique country.
>
> For most Americans, prayer is real and we sub-

ordinate ourselves to a God on whom we call for wisdom, guidance and salvation.

For most Americans, the prospect of a ruthlessly secular society that would forbid public reference to God and systematically remove all religious symbols from the public square is horrifying.

Yet the voice of the overwhelming majority of Americans is rejected by a media-academic-legal elite that finds religious expression frightening and threatening, or old-fashioned and unsophisticated.

It's getting pretty tiresome cataloging all the ways religious expression is under attack in America today. It seems like every Christmas brings another story of a crèche being banned from the front of a public building. When I was mayor of Wasilla, I had to fight for six Christmases to keep the baby Jesus manger scene on display on Wasilla Lake. And the Ten Commandments are becoming harder to find in American courthouses than unicorns.

Most Americans are honestly puzzled about why these religious displays are so darn controversial. The fact is that these challenges reflect more than just theoretical, legal, and constitutional differences. They are evidence of a profound cultural divide. As Newt has written, most Americans are people of faith. According to a 2008 Pew poll, 92 percent of Americans believe in God or a universal spirit, and more than half of us pray at least once a day. And yet we have an influential academic and legal elite that not only fails to share this belief, but seems actively hostile to it.

One of the cases Newt talks about in his book is the attempt to purge the words "under God" from the Pledge of Allegiance. Even though the individual at the center of the case—the atheist activist Michael Newdow—ultimately failed in his effort, the Pledge case is a good example of the differences between the views of the vast majority of Americans and those of much of the elite when it comes to religious expression.

In 2003, Newdow objected to his young daughter having the opportunity to pledge allegiance to "one nation, under God" in her public school classroom every morning. (Newdow never married his daughter's mother, who is raising the child to believe in God.) And even though the Supreme Court has ruled that students who object to the Pledge don't have to say it, Newdow insisted that the phrase "under God" was a violation of his right to transmit his atheist views to his daughter. So he brought a lawsuit, and the liberal Ninth Circuit Court, as is its wont, ruled that the Pledge was unconstitutional, although thankfully, in 2004, the Supreme Court reversed the ruling.

To understand the cultural issues at play in this case, a little history is necessary. Although the Pledge of Allegiance has been around since 1892, the words "under God" weren't added until 1954. They were added by bipartisan legislation after the minister at President Eisenhower's church said, in a sermon in which the president was present, "There [is] something missing in the pledge, [something that is] the characteristic and definitive factor in the American way of life." According to an article I found from that time, Congress was deluged with mail in favor of the change. Churches, veterans' groups, labor unions, and newspapers all got behind it. Not surprisingly, Congress approved the change by a unanimous vote.

Fast-forward fifty years, and liberal activists have decided that the result of this unanimous vote of Congress is somehow "divisive." The *New York Times*, writing in 2002, even called the 1954 change, undertaken in the midst of the U.S.-Soviet cold war rivalry, "a petty attempt to link patriotism with religious piety." Petty? I hear a lot of people these days talk about the cold war as though it were a paranoid fantasy of right-wing fanatics. But the differences between the United States and the Soviet Union were real—and consequential. One of those differences was belief in God. Communism is an explicitly atheist ideology. Congress's 1954 amendment to the Pledge wasn't "petty," it was a genuine expression, not just of patriotism, but of the unique aspect of American freedom: the belief that it is God-given and can't be legitimately taken away. Far from pandering to cold war paranoia, Congress was reminding America, and the world, of the wellspring of freedom.

Ronald Reagan made this point in the way only he could in his famous "evil empire" speech. Lost in all the hoopla over the American president using these words to describe the Soviet Union is the fact that Reagan's speech was devoted mostly to exploring faith in *American* life. The difference between our system of government and the Soviet system—one acknowledges God and the other doesn't—has significance beyond religion, Reagan reminded us. The way the two countries treated faith, he said, had direct consequences for how they treated their people. Where there was God, there was freedom. Where He was not recognized, there was tyranny.

During my first press conference as President, in answer to a direct question, I pointed out that, as good Marxist-Leninists, the Soviet leaders have openly and publicly declared that the only morality they recognize is that which will further their cause, which is world revolution. I think I should point out I was only quoting Lenin, their guiding spirit, who said in 1920 that they repudiate all morality that proceeds from supernatural ideas—that's their name for religion—or ideas that are outside class conceptions. Morality is entirely subordinate to the interests of class war. And everything is moral that is necessary for the annihilation of the old, exploiting social order and for uniting the proletariat.

Well, I think the refusal of many influential people to accept this elementary fact of Soviet doctrine illustrates an historical reluctance to see totalitarian powers for what they are. We saw this phenomenon in the 1930s. We see it too often today.

This doesn't mean we should isolate ourselves and refuse to seek an understanding with them . . . At the same time, however, they must be made to understand we will never compromise our principles and standards. We will never give away our freedom. We will never abandon our belief in God. . . .

Yes, let us pray for the salvation of all of those who live in totalitarian darkness—pray they will discover the joy of knowing God. But until they do, let us be aware that while they preach the supremacy of the state, declare its omnipotence over individual man, and predict its eventual domination of all peoples on the Earth, they are the focus of evil in the modern world.

Reagan got a lot of flak for that speech. But I wonder if the real problem for some wasn't that he called the Soviet system evil, but that he called ours *good*. After all, as Reagan said, the atheism of the Soviet system was right there in the writings and teachings of Lenin. What drove his critics crazy wasn't that Reagan pointed out the godlessness of the Soviet system, but that he pointed out the presence of God in ours. What they missed was that, by calling the Soviet system by its true name, he brought the Russian people themselves one step closer to freedom.

That, in the end, is the significance of the words "under God" in our Pledge of Allegiance. Not that they somehow divide an overwhelmingly observant nation or that they were added in a cynical act of cold war gamesmanship. The phrase "one nation under God" is significant because it puts our freedom beyond the reach of men who "preach the supremacy of the state." It puts our freedom in the hands of the Creator from whom it came, and that is a safe place indeed.

———

The question that comes back to me again and again when I hear people attack religion and religious expression is, Why? Why do they have to attack peaceful expressions of faith? What is so offensive about a baby in a manger? What is threatening about the Ten Commandments, a moral code that, by the way, Christianity, Judaism, and Islam, the religions that account for 97 percent of all American believers, recognize as the basis for living a good life? Why can't people just live and let live?

Part of the answer is the cultural divide between our governing elites and the mass of the American people. Most of those who write for the mainstream media and teach at universities and law schools don't share the religious faith of their fellow Americans. They seem to regard people who believe in God and regularly attend their church or synagogue as alien beings, people who are "largely poor, uneducated and easy to command," as the *Washington Post* once famously put it. Perhaps for this and other obvious reasons, I often refer to the conventional press as the "lame stream media." The truth is that we *are* alien—to them.

Recently, columnist Jonah Goldberg hilariously channeled the mind-set of the mainstream media when it comes to covering conservatives, including religious conservatives. In its eyes, he writes, we come from another planet:

It's that shadowy, often-sinister world where carbon-based life forms of a generally humanoid appearance say and do things relating to, and supportive of, conservative causes and the Republican Party. These strange creatures have been observed using complex tools, caring and nurturing their young and even participating in complex social rituals. Most worship an unseen sky god that traces its roots back to the ancient Middle East. Even more astounding, these creatures are having a noticeable impact on American politics.

Aside from this cultural distance, there is a simpler (and more troubling) explanation for the new liberal intolerance. Today's secular elites don't agree with appeals to religion because they generally don't support the *reasons* for these appeals. Americans typically invoke faith in the public debate to support the sanctity of life, the preservation of marriage, and the nature of our freedom. Many liberals don't support these things, so they regard bringing faith into the argument as somehow unfair or intolerant—or just beside the point. Of course, they're happy to talk the God talk (if not walk the God walk) when it's for a cause they believe in. Witness House Speaker Nancy Pelosi insisting that she will pursue public policies consistent with the

"Word" of the Gospel, even as she votes against banning partial-birth abortion.

Another example of talking the (God) talk but not walking the walk among politicians occurred in the 2004 presidential debates between George W. Bush and John Kerry. In the final debate, both candidates spoke at length about the role of religion in their lives. President Bush was consistent in his belief, as he said, that "prayer and religion sustain me." But Senator Kerry changed his tune depending on the policy in question. On the issue of abortion, Kerry insisted, "I can't legislate or transfer to another American citizen my article of faith. What is an article of faith for me is not something that I can legislate on somebody who doesn't share that article of faith."

Fair enough. But then the topic shifted to government programs for the poor and the environment, and Kerry changed his tune. His faith, he said, was "why I fight against poverty. That's why I fight to clean up the environment and protect this earth. That's why I fight for equality and justice. All of those things come out of that fundamental teaching and belief of faith."

I know, I know. Politicians speaking out of both sides of their mouths. What a shocker! But this kind of hypocrisy when it comes to religion is widespread on the left, inside and outside Washington. After consistently calling any involvement of religion in politics offensive and unconstitutional, the *New York Times* suddenly applauded in 2006 when Cardinal Roger Mahony called on Catholics to engage in civil disobedience to protest a restrictionist immigration bill. In an editorial remarkably headlined "The Gospel vs. H.R. 4437," the *New York Times* editors discovered a newfound love of religion in political debate:

> The enormous influx of illegal immigrants and the lack of a coherent federal policy to handle it have prompted a jumble of responses by state and local governments, stirred the passions of the nativist fringe, and reinforced anxieties since 9/11. Cardinal Mahony's defiance adds a moral dimension to what has largely been a debate about politics and economics. "As his disciples, we are called to attend to the last, littlest, lowest and least in society and in the church," he said. . . .
>
> Cardinal Mahony's declaration of solidarity with illegal immigrants, for whom Lent is every day, is a startling call to civil disobedience, as courageous as it is timely.

Remarkable! Imagine the *Times* invoking the Gospel in defense of helping poor kids go to inner city Catholic schools (otherwise known as "school choice") or a pro-life nurse's right not to be required to assist at an abortion over the dictates of her conscience.

The question for so-called progressives, then, is: Which is it? Is it enlightened to talk about religion in the pursuit of liberal causes but constitutionally suspect when traditional American values are being defended? The fact is that religious faith has been invoked in every American movement of conscience, from the abolition of slavery to the prohibition of alcohol to the civil rights movement. Why is bringing faith into the argument good for thee but not for me?

Neither John Kerry nor the *New York Times* has any problem with the fact that the movements for the abolition of slavery and for civil rights were based on explicit appeals to Judeo-Christian morality. Such movements were led by clergy, and their rhetoric was infused with religious imagery. When Martin Luther King, Jr., was jailed for taking part in a nonviolent protest against racial segregation in Alabama in 1963, his famous "Letter from Birmingham Jail" was both a refutation of racial segregation and a repudiation of those who opposed civil disobedience in pursuit of civil rights—a *refudiation*, if you will—cast in explicitly religious terms. It is an eloquent letter that all Americans should read. "An unjust law is a human law that is not rooted in eternal law and natural law," he wrote:

I am in Birmingham because injustice is here. Just as the prophets of the eighth century B.C. left their villages and carried their "thus saith the Lord" far beyond the boundaries of their home towns, and just as the Apostle Paul left his village of Tarsus and carried the gospel of Jesus Christ to the far corners of the Greco-Roman world, so am I compelled to carry the gospel of freedom beyond my own home town. Like Paul, I must constantly respond to the Macedonian call for aid.

King wrote his letter in response to white clergy who had urged him to carry on the civil rights struggle in the courts and not in the streets. But King defended the civil rights protestors as unsung "children of God" who were "standing up for what is best in the American dream and for the most sacred values in our Judaeo-Christian heritage."

I wish you had commended the Negro sit-inners and demonstrators of Birmingham for their sublime courage, their willingness to suffer and their amazing discipline in the midst of great provocation. One day the South will recognize its real heroes. They will be the James Merediths, with the noble sense of purpose that enables them to face jeering, and hostile mobs, and with the agonizing loneliness that characterizes the life of the pioneer. They will be old, oppressed, battered Negro women, symbolized in a seventy-two-year-old woman in Montgomery, Alabama, who rose up with a sense of dignity and with her people decided not to ride segregated buses, and who responded with ungrammatical profundity to one who inquired about her weariness: "My feet is tired, but my soul is rested." They will be the young high school and college students, the young ministers of the gospel and a host of their elders, courageously and nonviolently sitting in at lunch counters and willingly going to jail for conscience's sake. One day the South will know that when these disinherited children of God sat down at lunch counters, they were in reality standing up for what is best in the American dream and for the most sacred values in our Judaeo-Christian heritage, and thusly carrying our nation back to those great wells of democracy which were dug deep by the founding fathers in their formulation of the Constitution and the Declaration of Independence.

Martin Luther King, Jr.'s, appeal to our religious faith and the morality that it informs eventually succeeded, and thank God for that. Just as our Founders couldn't foresee America surviving in liberty without religion, it's hard to see how slavery could have been abolished and civil rights achieved in an America without religious faith and values. No one objected to the civil rights movement's grounding in Christianity, seeing it as somehow offensive to Americans of other faiths, let alone harmful to atheists. People understood that King was appealing to what was best in us, both as Americans and as human beings.

And yet this selective evocation of religious tolerance continues today when Americans are lectured about who can exercise their freedom of religion, and under what circumstances. The plan to build a mosque just steps from Ground Zero in New York is a good example.

New York mayor Michael Bloomberg and other supporters of the initiative have argued that not allowing a mosque to be built at a sacred site where nearly three thousand people lost their lives in the name of radical Islam would somehow violate American principles of tolerance and openness.

I agree with the sister of one of the 9/11 victims (and a New York resident) who said, "This is a place which is six hundred feet from where almost three thousand people were torn to pieces by Islamic extremists. I think that it is incredibly insensitive and audacious really for them to build a mosque, not only on that site, but to do it specifically so that they could be in proximity to where that atrocity happened."

Many Americans, me included, feel it would be an intolerable and tragic mistake to allow such a project to go forward on this hallowed ground. Of course the supporters of this project have a constitutional right to build a mosque on private land. But just because they *can* do something doesn't mean they necessarily should. This is nothing close to "religious intolerance"; it's what our Founders called "a decent respect for the opinions of mankind"—or in this case, their fellow Americans.

It must be frustrating to those who want to ban religion from the American public square to see our country turn, time and again, to prayer in our moments of need. Since before there was an America, our leaders have met moments of challenge and adversity with appeals to God for guidance, strength, and wisdom. They have spoken, not just for themselves, but for the nation. They have been Democrats and Republicans, devout and less observant, regular churchgoing and CEO (Christmas and Easter Only). Even as early as the Constitutional Convention, Benjamin Franklin beseeched his fellow delegates to "appl[y] to the Father of lights to illuminate our understandings" when the Convention deadlocked on the issue of congressional representations:

In the beginning of the Contest with G. Britain, when we were sensible of danger we had daily prayer in this room for the divine protection.— Our prayers, Sir, were heard, & they were graciously answered. All of us who were engaged in the struggle must have observed frequent instances of a superintending providence in our favor.

To that kind providence we owe this happy opportunity of consulting in peace on the means of establishing our future national felicity. And have we now forgotten that powerful friend? Or do we imagine that we no longer need his assistance? I have lived, Sir, a long time, and the longer I live, the more convincing proofs I see of this truth— that God Governs in the affairs of men. And if a sparrow cannot fall to the ground without his notice, is it probable that an empire can rise without his aid?

This propensity to seek the guidance and blessing of our Creator makes us unique among Western nations.

Supreme Court Justice Antonin Scalia tells of hearing about the 9/11 attacks when he was in Rome attending an international conference of judges and lawyers:

> That night and the next morning virtually all of the participants watched, in their hotel rooms, the address to the nation by the President of the United States concerning the murderous attacks upon the Twin Towers and the Pentagon, in which thousands of Americans had been killed. The address ended, as Presidential addresses often do, with the prayer "God bless America." The next afternoon I was approached by one of the judges from a European country, who, after extending his profound condolences for my country's loss, sadly observed, "How I wish that the Head of State of my country, at a similar time of national tragedy and distress, could conclude his address 'God bless _____.' It is of course absolutely forbidden."

George W. Bush was often attacked as a "theocrat" or a "Christian fascist" for his unapologetic evocation of his faith. But prayer by American leaders in times of crisis is routine, bipartisan, and good.

I remember well President Bush's stirring words at the National Cathedral on September 14, 2001. It seemed the most natural thing in the world for Americans to pray on that day. And our commander in chief led us with reassurance and eloquence:

Our purpose as a nation is firm, yet our wounds as a people are recent and unhealed and lead us to pray. In many of our prayers this week, there's a searching and an honesty. At St. Patrick's Cathedral in New York, on Tuesday, a woman said, "I pray to God to give us a sign that he's still here."

Others have prayed for the same, searching hospital to hospital, carrying pictures of those still missing. God's signs are not always the ones we look for. We learn in tragedy that his purposes are not always our own, yet the prayers of private suffering, whether in our homes or in this great cathedral are known and heard and understood.

There are prayers that help us last through the day or endure the night. There are prayers of friends and strangers that give us strength for the journey, and there are prayers that yield our will to a will greater than our own.

This world He created is of moral design. Grief and tragedy and hatred are only for a time. Goodness, remembrance and love have no end, and the Lord of life holds all who die and all who mourn.

"The prayers of private suffering . . . are known and heard and understood." How I clung to those words in those frightening days. It was not the first time America had faced a crisis, of course. Fifty-seven years earlier, in 1944, another president—a Democrat president—had prayed with America in its time of need. On the evening of June 6, 1944, as Allied troops battled and died on the beaches of France following the Normandy invasion, FDR led the nation in prayer. And it wasn't just a speech with a casual reference to the Almighty. It was a full-throated, on-your-knees prayer to a national radio audience estimated at one hundred million, making it, according to some, the largest single mass prayer of all time. Here is what Roosevelt said:

> Last night when I spoke with you about the fall of Rome, I knew at that moment that troops of the United States and our Allies were crossing the Channel in another and greater operation. It has come to pass with success thus far.
>
> And so, in this poignant hour, I ask you to join with me in prayer:
>
> Almighty God: our sons, pride of our Nation, this day have set upon a mighty endeavor, a struggle to preserve our Republic, our religion, and our civilization, and to set free a suffering humanity.

Lead them straight and true; give strength to their arms, stoutness to their hearts, steadfastness in their faith.

They will need Thy blessings. Their road will be long and hard. For the enemy is strong. He may hurl back our forces. Success may not come with rushing speed, but we shall return again and again; and we know that by Thy grace, and by the righteousness of our cause, our sons will triumph.

They will be sore tried, by night and by day, without rest—until the victory is won. The darkness will be rent by noise and flame. Men's souls will be shaken with the violences of war.

For these men are lately drawn from the ways of peace. They fight not for the lust of conquest. They fight to end conquest. They fight to liberate. They fight to let justice arise, and tolerance and good will among all Thy people. They yearn but for the end of battle, for their return to the haven of home.

Some will never return. Embrace these, Father, and receive them, Thy heroic servants, into Thy kingdom.

And for us at home—fathers, mothers, children, wives, sisters and brothers of brave men overseas, whose thoughts and prayers are ever with them—help us, Almighty God, to rededicate ourselves in renewed faith in Thee in this hour of great sacrifice.

Many people have urged that I call the Nation into a single day of special prayer. But because the road is long and the desire is great, I ask that our people devote themselves in a continuance of prayer. As we rise to each new day, and again when each day is spent, let words of prayer be on our lips, invoking Thy help to our efforts.

Give us strength, too—strength in our daily tasks, to redouble the contributions we make in the physical and the material support of our armed forces.

And let our hearts be stout, to wait out the long travail, to bear sorrows that may come, to impart our courage unto our sons wheresoever they may be.

And, O Lord, give us faith. Give us faith in Thee; faith in our sons; faith in each other; faith in our united crusade. Let not the keenness of our spirit ever be dulled. Let not the impacts of temporary events, of temporal matters of but fleeting moment—let not these deter us in our unconquerable purpose.

With Thy blessing, we shall prevail over the

unholy forces of our enemy. Help us to conquer
the apostles of greed and racial arrogancies. Lead
us to the saving of our country, and with our sister
nations into a world unity that will spell a sure
peace—a peace invulnerable to the schemings of
unworthy men. And a peace that will let all men
live in freedom, reaping the just rewards of their
honest toil. Thy will be done, Almighty God.
Amen.

Ronald Reagan once quoted Abraham Lincoln as
saying, "I have been driven many times to my knees by
the overwhelming conviction that I had nowhere else to
go."

I know the feeling.

I pray all the time. I always have. Saying a prayer
was the first thing I did when I learned I was going
to have my first child and it was the last thing I did
before I stepped out in front of more than forty million
viewers to give my speech at the 2008 Republican National Convention. I asked God to crush my "self" and
give me His strength and grace for that time. I asked
Todd and our kids to join me in prayer, seeking not
self-glorification but an opportunity to freely express
what I believed God had put in my heart to share. I
also turned to prayer backstage at the vice-presidential

debate in 2008, although Piper scolded me for "cheating" when I asked her to pray with me that God would have His way and His words at the event that night!

And I'm not alone in my reliance on prayer. We are a prayerful country. What's more, I think it's significant that we pray not just in times of danger or crisis, such as during the Normandy invasion or the 9/11 attacks, but in quieter times as well. We pray for inspiration and guidance, and also pray in thanksgiving and gratitude. We even have a quintessentially American holiday, Thanksgiving, devoted to precisely that purpose.

I recently came across a collection of American prayers that shows the many ways we turn to our Creator to thank Him, to remember Him—and sometimes, to beg for His help.

One prayer is from a genuine American hero, Harriet Tubman. What a thrill it was for me to visit her home in rural New York a couple of years ago. As the collection notes, Harriet Tubman was called a "nineteenth-century Moses" because she was once a slave, and when she found her freedom, she devoted her life to freeing others. She never lost a person while helping them make their escape on the Underground Railroad, and she credited her faith for her success. Here's the brief prayer she would say as she began one of her daring rescues: "I'm going to hold steady on You, an'

You've got to see me through." It says something that a remarkable woman like Harriet Tubman—a woman courageous enough to defy slavery and strong enough to save hundreds of her fellow men and women via the Underground Railroad—would put her faith and fate so blithely in God's hands. Her wonderful little prayer is a good reminder to those of us with less courage and less strength that we can accomplish more if we just do the same.

Another of my favorite prayers is also a poem (or is it a poem that is also a prayer?) by Emily Dickinson. It's a simple, logical explanation for a faith that is as deeply felt as it is unproved—and unprovable.

> *I never saw a moor,*
> *I never saw the sea;*
> *Yet know I how the heather looks,*
> *And what a wave must be.*
>
> *I never spoke with God,*
> *Nor visited in heaven;*
> *Yet certain am I of the spot*
> *As if the chart were given.*

Another prayer I really love, believe it or not, was one Elvis Presley reportedly used to say. The story goes that before every performance he would find a quiet place offstage and say this one-line prayer: "Send me some light—I need it."

Pretty much says it all, eh!

But my favorite in this wonderful collection is a prayer that is as modest, wide-open, unassuming, and free as this country. Fittingly, it's called "A Cowboy's Prayer." It was written by Badger Clark, who was later named the first poet laureate of South Dakota. I love this prayer for its gratitude for freedom, its honest appreciation for hard work, and for its author's simple yearning to be a better man:

O Lord, I've never run where churches grow,
I've always loved Creation better as it stood
That day you finished it, so long ago,
And looked upon your work, and found it good.
I know that others might find You in the light
That's sifted down through tinted window panes,
And yet I seem to feel You near tonight.

Let me be easy on the man that's down
And make me square and generous with all;
I'm careless sometimes, Lord, when I'm in town
But never let them call me mean or small.
Make me as big and open as the plains,
As honest as the hoss between my knees,
Clean as the wind that blows behind the rains,
Free as the hawk that circles down the breeze!

I thank you, Lord, that I am placed so well,
That you made my freedom so complete;
That I'm no slave to whistle, clock or bell,
Nor weak-eyed prisoner of wall and street.
Just let me live my life as I've begun
And give me work that is open to the sky;

Make me a pardner of the wind and sun,
And I won't ask for a life that's soft or high.

Forgive me, Lord, if sometimes I forget.
You know about the reasons that are hid.
You understand the things that gall and fret;
You know me better than my mother did.
Just keep an eye on all that's done and said
And right me, sometimes, when I turn aside,
And guide me on the long, dim trail ahead
That stretches upward toward the Great Divide.

Whether it's a cross in a desert or a prayer in a time of national crisis, evidence abounds that America is a deeply faithful country. That doesn't mean we're all the same religion or even all regular churchgoers. I think a lot of us feel the same as the cowboy: We see God in the beauty of mountains and lakes and the other glories of His creation, not necessarily always through stained-glass windows. I know Alaskans can relate. We see God in Mt. McKinley, our majestic glacial carvings, and the breathtaking vistas right outside our front doors. And we look to our Creator, not just for our freedom, but to be better men and women. It's a pity that some have a problem with that. But as for me, I'm going to continue to seek God's blessings. I need Him to "right me . . . when I turn aside." And to guide me on that "long, dim trail" that stretches "upward toward the Great Divide."

Nine

OUR NORTH STAR

I was very pregnant with Trig when Todd and I took a rare few hours between official events on a Saturday in March 2008 and went to the movies. We had just attended the start of the Iditarod sled dog race in Anchorage, so we decided to thaw out inside a warm movie theater before attending a town hall meeting. The movie we watched was *Juno*.

There's a scene from this memorable movie that I think says a lot about how many of us experience our faith. You'll recall that the movie is about a young girl,

Juno, who finds herself pregnant at sixteen. She goes on to have the baby and put it up for adoption. And because she chooses to have the baby, when the movie came out there was a lot of talk about whether *Juno* had a pro-life message. Some insisted that it did, while others objected just as stridently that there was no anti-abortion theme.

I remember thinking that both sides got it wrong. There was no preaching, in-your-face message about abortion in the movie, either pro or con. Director Jason Reitman was subtler and, I think, more clever than that. The scene in which Juno ultimately chooses not to have an abortion shows how.

From the moment she finds out she's pregnant it seems like a foregone conclusion that Juno will, as she says, "nip" her problem "in the bud." And sure enough, she makes an appointment and goes to a clinic. There's an abortion protestor outside whom Juno basically ignores. But just as Juno is about to enter the clinic, the young, sweet protestor says something that seems to affect her. She yells, "Your baby has fingernails!" And Juno pauses. She continues into the clinic, but you can tell she's struggling. Inside, she sees the heavily pierced receptionist texting as she monotones a greeting and asks Juno to fill out a form. "Don't skip the hairy details," the receptionist says, bored. "We need to know about every score and every sore." Then she offers Juno a free condom, boysenberry-flavored. Juno can't take it. She leaves. "I'm staying pregnant," she tells her friend.

You could argue (as some did) that there wouldn't be much of a story to tell in *Juno* if she had an abortion in the first fifteen minutes—certainly nothing very funny. But it strikes me that the reason she rethinks her automatic decision to have an abortion—hearing that her baby has fingernails—sends a very understated but powerful message. Despite all the rhetoric designed to make abortion just another "choice" that Juno and her friends grew up with, she ultimately recognizes that there is a living being growing inside her. It is a life she didn't ask for. It is an inconvenient life at the time. But it is a life nonetheless. She just can't bring herself to destroy it once she imagines it as something human, as opposed to an abstract "problem" to be "solved" by a routine medical procedure.

Most Americans, I think, are a lot like Juno. They don't think in ideological or political terms about their religious faith. They may not even be actively religious at all—but they still want to do the right thing, and they want to see others do the right thing as well. Our culture encourages this by doing something unique and, I think, highly exceptional: it takes fundamentally religious values such as the sanctity of life and secularizes them without surrendering their morality. America has a special ability to take the truths and moral lessons of religion and put them to work in ways that benefit everyone, regardless of their faith.

I don't know what Jason Reitman's religion or his politics are—and it doesn't matter. He made a pretty great movie with a subtle but powerful message that I recognize from my faith. Maybe others see it, too; maybe they don't. But everyone who sees the movie understands that Juno makes a moral choice. She doesn't act in accordance with anyone's politics but according to the dictates of her own conscience. And the morality that informs that conscience is found in the great religious traditions of America.

Reitman isn't alone in sneaking traditional messages into his work. I've been tough on Hollywood in this book, but I'm also a fan of director Judd Apatow's films. Movies such as *Knocked Up* (in which a young woman becomes a mom thanks to a one-night stand with a slacker) and *The Forty-Year-Old Virgin* (self-explanatory!) deliver the same subversive moral messages that can be found in *Juno*. The uniquely American twist is that the morality served up by these movies is a side dish that comes with a main course of bawdy frat house humor. *New York Times* columnist Ross Douthat agrees: "No contemporary figure has done more than Apatow, the 41-year-old auteur of gross-out comedies, to rebrand social conservatism for a younger generation that associates it primarily with priggishness and puritanism."

When people like Douthat point out these moral messages, critics usually reply that such moralism is necessary to sell tickets in America. But that objection just makes my point. For all that is rotten in our popular culture, it seems clear (at least to me) that there is still a fundamental desire on the part of most people, at least some of the time, to be uplifted by our public entertainment. We don't want to be preached to. Sometimes we just want to laugh and be distracted for a couple of hours from the cares and worries of our daily lives (which is why some of us love to watch sports, too!). But we also want to see our values reinforced and not mocked or belittled on the big screen. Americans stayed away in droves from the bumper crop of anti–Iraq War movies put out by Hollywood in the last couple of years for precisely this reason. The success of filmmakers such as Jason Reitman and Judd Apatow is due to the fact that they believe entertainment can accommodate this moral impulse.

A European movie might have had Juno get her abortion in the opening scene and then spend the next hour and fifteen minutes smoking cigarettes and pondering the meaning of life. It would have been depressing *and* boring. Not here. Americans want to be entertained, but we also want to see people do the right thing, even when it's hard and there is no prospect of being rewarded. Hooray for some in Hollywood for occasionally letting us see that.

There are many other things about America that prove my point that you don't have to share my faith to benefit from what faith has given America. As the recent release of the original text of the *Big Book* illustrates, Alcoholics Anonymous is a great example of how religious values (by another name) have helped millions of Americans.

True story: Alcoholics Anonymous actually grew out of a religion-based recovery program called the Oxford Group. It was started in 1935, in the middle of the Great Depression, by a down-on-his-luck alcoholic named Bill Wilson who had a conversion experience in a hospital room while drying out from one of his many binges. By Wilson's own account, he was engulfed by a white light and God revealed himself to him. He never drank again. He joined the Oxford Group, a Protestant movement of mainly elite Americans trying to recover from addictions. But he quickly broke away and helped create AA in order to attract Catholics and more main-stream Americans. He borrowed directly from religion and psychology to create the famous Twelve Steps. Wilson settled on twelve, he said, because there were twelve apostles.

Born of a religious conversion, AA has become a creed of personal salvation open to all. It is a secular church of self-help. No other recovery program has helped so many so successfully as this one, which famously calls on participants to begin their journey to recovery by surrendering to "a higher power." You don't have to be religious to join AA; you just have to have the desire to stop drinking. But it is the elements it borrows from faith that make the program work.

Even Americans who've never had a problem with alcohol or drugs are familiar with many of the Twelve Steps—that's how widespread they have become. They begin by asking participants to admit their powerlessness before their addiction, recognize a greater power that can help them, make amends for past mistakes, learn a new way of life and, critically, help others who are suffering in the same way. All people of faith will recognize the ethical teachings of religion (and not just Christianity) in AA's Twelve Steps. In short, AA says to its participants, *You're not strong enough to carry this burden by yourself. You need help. Help is here.* That's the feeling I have every time I hit my knees and pray. As a matter of fact, I keep a copy of AA's famous "Serenity Prayer" taped inside a favorite devotional book. I glance at it occasionally and am reminded of the connectivity it creates among all:

> *God, grant me the serenity*
> *To accept the things I cannot change;*
> *Courage to change the things I can;*
> *And wisdom to know the difference.*

The greatest proof of the success of AA is the army of imitators it has spawned. Hundreds of self-help groups use Twelve Step principles to help millions of addicts and their friends and family deal with everything from drug abuse to problem gambling, overeating, and even borrowing too much. If it's easier for Americans of diverse faith traditions, as well as agnostics and atheists, to acknowledge a "higher power" than it is to invoke the name of God, so be it. The important point is that the Twelve Steps work—and we seem to need them now more than ever.

The diseases treated by these programs can be too often traced to the bad effects on our society of secularism and its corrosive ideology. It's an ironic (but very American) twist that we have used a secularized version of religion to try to cure them.

Former attorney general John Ashcroft—a deeply devout Christian—used to say something I agree with wholeheartedly: "It's against my religion to impose my religion on others." What our culture does when it translates religious values into secular terms and applies them to useful ends isn't about brainwashing or trying to convert anyone—quite the opposite. It's a way of conferring a rich moral heritage while respecting everyone's religious freedom.

All the great religions call on us to follow the Golden Rule: to treat others as we would like to be treated ourselves. Call me biased, but one of the best ways America follows this faith value in a secular way is in the treatment we give to individuals with special needs. Without so much as mentioning religion, we strive to treat these most vulnerable members of our society the way we ourselves would like to be treated.

I often speak to families with special needs kids. The room is inevitably noisy because the kids are running around being kids. I tell my audience not to worry and not to hush them—"That's the sound of life"—and I just talk louder.

That these amazing moms and dads just chuckle and listen harder says so much about them. Their children aren't easy. I know from experience that the overwhelming emotion parents have when they learn they will have a child with special needs is fear: fear that caring for a special child is too hard; fear that their marriages and their pocketbooks and their hearts won't be able to handle it. Simply through the act of allowing their children to be born, the parents I meet are telling us something significant about themselves. Either that their belief in God gave them the courage to choose life, as it did for me, or that something in their hearts just told them to hold on and have faith, that they could handle it.

They are truly remarkable people. And although I, too, have a son with more challenges than many of us will ever encounter, I don't count myself among their number. I am blessed with so much to support me—a wonderful, involved husband, a strong family, a caring community, and the resources we need to provide for Trig. So many of the families I meet aren't nearly as materially blessed as we are, and yet they held on to faith and chose life. They would never approve of the term, but they're truly heroes.

We could always do more, but America says a lot about itself in the way we support these amazing families. Not just with laws such as the Americans with Disabilities Act, but in our private lives; in countless individual gestures in countless communities, our faith-rooted values are put to work to help special kids and adults.

For example, I read about a special education teacher in the tiny fishing village of Port Washington, Wisconsin, who wanted to build a playground for kids with special needs. She asked her kids what they wanted to have on it. "They all said pirate ships," she said. When she found out that the project would cost nearly $1.5 million, she almost gave up. But the citizens of Port Washington came together to make it happen. A design firm provided instructions. Businesses donated materials. Citizens gave of their money and their time. In the end, 2,800 people—a third of the town—pitched in to build the playground. Today it is a wonderland for all kinds of kids—and complete with a giant rocking pirate ship!

An American who is responsible, maybe more than any other, for challenging the low expectations we used to have of kids with special needs is Eunice Kennedy Shriver. As a child, this deeply compassionate woman had witnessed a society that did not live out its values in dealing with her mentally challenged sister, Rosemary. In those days, Americans like Rosemary were often locked away in asylums and sometimes subjected to inhumane medical procedures. Mrs. Shriver wanted to open the doors of the possible to all kids with mental

268 · SARAH PALIN

and physical challenges. So in 1968, just seven weeks after her brother Bobby was killed by an assassin's bullet, she held the first Special Olympics in Chicago. I love the message she used to open the games:

> In ancient Rome, the gladiators went into the arena with these words on their lips: "Let me win, but if I cannot win, let me be brave in the attempt."
>
> Today, all of you young athletes are in the arena. Many of you will win, but even more important, I know you will be brave and bring credit to your parents and to your country. Let us begin the Olympics.

It's true that America loves winners, but there's one thing we love more: competitors who are brave in the attempt. I think that's why we all have such admiration for the kids with special challenges who come out to compete and have a little fun in the process. Our natural human desire to help others and see them succeed is translated easily to the playing field. Competition and hard work give all of us that sense of worth and dignity that all God's children crave. And when someone with special needs not only tries hard, but tries hard and succeeds, we are all lifted up. One family I met told me about a deaf baseball player—the wonderfully named Curtis Pride—who proves the point.

Before he was five months old, Curtis's parents knew something was wrong. But even after doctors diagnosed him with 95 percent hearing loss, they were determined that their boy not feel different. So they enrolled six-year-old Curtis in a local T-ball league. His first time at bat he hit the ball over the center fielder's head and rounded the bases so quickly he passed the runner ahead of him between first and second base. What Curtis didn't know about the rules of T-ball he more than made up for in talent and enthusiasm. He was hooked.

Curtis Pride became a standout high school athlete, graduated with a basketball scholarship at William and Mary, and was a draft pick by the New York Mets. He split his time between college and Major League Baseball until he graduated, when he began to play full time on a Mets farm club. After languishing for a time there, he went to the Montreal Expos farm club. He worked his way up through the system until one day his big break came. *Reader's Digest*, in the way only the *Reader's Digest* can, told the story of Pride's first scoring hit in the major leagues:

Curt Pride was startled when Montreal Expos manager Felipe Alou yelled out his name. The Philadelphia Phillies were leading Montreal 7–4 in the seventh inning. With one out and two runners on base, Pride thought Alou would send in a more experienced pinch hitter. But Alou was calling him.

In his first time at bat a few days before, Pride had driven the ball deep to right. "I can hit Major League pitching!" he told his parents. Now his old friend Steve Grupe was in the stands to watch him play, and his new team was depending on him.

Bobby Thigpen, the Phillies' flame-throwing relief pitcher, was on the mound. As Pride gripped the bat, Thigpen fired a hard slider. Pride waited; then at the last moment his bat exploded across the plate. The ball shot like a bullet between the outfielders and bounced all the way to the wall.

Racing around first, Pride slid into second in a cloud of dust. Safe! Both runners scored! In the stands, Steve Grupe leapt up, pummeled the air with his fists and whooped.

Excited, Pride looked to third-base coach Jerry Manuel to see if he had the green light to steal on the next pitch. But Manuel was motioning to the stands. Pride looked up. All 45,000 fans were on their feet, stamping and cheering.

As Pride stood, frozen, the thunderous ovation continued. Manuel, tears welling in his eyes, motioned for Curt to doff his cap.

Then, as the stamping and cheering reached a

crescendo, something incredible happened. It started as a vibrating rumble, then grew more intense until, for the first time in his life, Curt Pride actually heard people cheering for him. The silent curtain that had separated him from his dream had parted.

Consider it sappy, perhaps, but we may as well admit it: we love these kinds of stories. And how we treat the most vulnerable—the unborn, the disabled, the aged— says something fundamental about us as a country. It's a question not just of faith in God, but of respect for the inherent dignity of every human being. Curtis Pride's story is a remarkable reflection on him, but it's also a pretty good reflection on the society that helped make it happen.

Speaking for myself, I find that my faith guides me in ways large and small, consciously and unconsciously, virtually nonstop. And I've found some great resources for even the most mundane aspects of life's journey. In fact, our culture has produced a vast array of inspirational books and other resources that draw on our rich religious heritage.

When I was in Georgia recently, Dr. Charles Stanley gave me one of his many books, *How to Reach Your Full*

Potential for God. It sounds pretty heavy, but it's full of helpful advice and wise counsel that can be applied to many of the situations I find myself in every day.

Here is Dr. Stanley on using your time wisely:

> [One] important challenge you face is the way you order your time. A balanced schedule will help you be the person God wants you to be and do the things He wants you to do. YOUR TIME IS YOUR LIFE. TIME IS IRREVERSIBLE. IT IS IRREPLACEABLE . . . When you reach the age of 70, you will have lived 840 months. That's 25,550 days or 613,200 hours or 36,792,000 minutes . . . every bit of that time is holy because it is a gift from a holy God. It is to be valued and spent in ways that honor the Giver. . . . Think of time as an investment.

It's so important to remember that every day is a gift, especially when we feel pulled in too many directions and asked to do too many things. Dr. Stanley also taught me a great tip on how to tell the difference between the truly important and the merely urgent.

If something is presented to you as "you must decide right now or the opportunity ends," take that as a sign that your answer should be no. An opportunity tied to a rushed or ironclad ultimatum is rarely from God.

If I had listened to what other people said about what I should do and how I should invest my energies in life, I cannot begin to fathom all that I might have missed or lost.

Had I listened to those who were skeptical that a simple Alaskan housewife and hockey mom could run for public office, I would never have had the opportunity to serve as a mayor, a commissioner, a governor, and a national vice-presidential candidate.

Had I listened to those who suggested it would be political suicide to hand the Governor's reins over to my lieutenant governor entering my lame duck last year in office—a choice I made so that I could fight for Alaska, and America, more effectively in a different venue—then my state would have suffered from the obstruction and paralysis of my office by the politically motivated attacks that began the day I was announced as the Republican vice-presidential candidate in 2008.

Had I listened to the politicos (even some within my own political action committee) and shied away from endorsing candidates I knew were best for America—people such as Susana Martinez, Nikki Haley, Doug

Hoffman, Joe Miller, and Karen Handel—I wouldn't have been using my position in the best interests of the country I love.

I might also add that had I listened to the voices in our culture telling me that I should spare myself the trouble and heartache of bringing a child with special needs into the world, our family would have missed out on the most positive and life-changing thing ever to happen for us.

It's quite bold of people we don't even know, and who don't really know us, to tell us what's best for our careers, our families, and our future. Charles Stanley's book reminds us that God did not put us on earth to have people pull us this way and that so we could do things for their benefit, their advancement, and their goals:

> Certainly, we are to work with one another and help one another the best we can. But no person is to be the "author and finisher" of our lives apart from God. He has a wonderful way of weaving together everyone's personal plans and purposes. When things function according to His will, people are helping one another even as they are working with or for one another.
>
> But at the same time that we aren't meant to be

anyone's slave or puppet, we are also called by our faith to understand that the purposes of life are much bigger than us and our private concerns.

Though this message is emphasized by all the great religious traditions, it also comes down to us from secular sources. I don't claim to be a scholar of ancient Greek philosophy, but Plato is supposed to have said, "Be kind, for everyone you meet is fighting a hard battle."

Whoever said it, the statement has the ring of profound truth. Our nature as humans is to be so self-absorbed that we must discipline ourselves to remember that every day, and in many ways, we yield to the changing nature of the universe. Conditions and circumstances ebb and flow, sometimes in our favor, sometimes in a way that upsets our plans or challenges our perception of the way things ought to be. Until we step outside ourselves and realize that change is inevitable for everyone, and that everyone is thus engaged in some kind of challenge, we can become overwhelmed by our own struggles. A constantly changing cosmos is the cause.

Max Lucado's easy, clever, and inspiring book *It's Not About Me* talks about how humanity came to this (difficult) realization:

Blame the bump on Copernicus. Until Copernicus came along in 1543, we earthlings enjoyed center stage.

Ah, the hub of the planetary wheel, the navel of the heavenly body, the 1600 Pennsylvania Avenue of the cosmos. Ptolemy's second-century finding convinced us. Stick a pin in the center of the stellar map, you've found the earth. Dead center.

And, what's more, dead still! Let the other planets vagabond through the skies. Not us. No sir. We stay put . . . But then came Nicolaus. Nicolaus Copernicus with his maps, drawings, bony nose, Polish accent, and pestering questions.

"Ahem, can anyone tell me what causes the seasons to change? Why do some stars appear in the day and others at night? Does anyone know exactly how far ships can sail before falling off the edge of the earth?"

"Trivialities!" people scoffed. "Who has time for such problems? Smile and wave, everyone. Heaven's homecoming queen has more pressing matters to which to attend."

But Copernicus persisted, Lucado reminds us.

He tapped our collective shoulders and cleared his throat. "Forgive my proclamation, but," and

pointing a lone finger toward the sun, he announced, "behold the center of the solar system."

For over half a century people denied Copernicus's
findings of fact. And when like-minded Galileo came
along, Lucado reports that the throne locked him up
and the Church kicked him out! "You'd have thought
he had called the pope a Baptist," Lucado observed.
"People didn't take well to demotions back then."

Well, we still don't. Again, from *It's Not About
Me*:

What Copernicus did for the earth, God does for
our souls. Tapping the collective shoulder of humanity, He points to the Son—His Son—and says,
"Behold the center of it all."

As individual human beings created to participate
in and contribute to good on the third rock from the
sun, we'd do well to quit thinking we're the center of it
all—the center of our circle of friends, our office, our
softball team, our political party. No, we are part of a
much larger body. The sooner we grasp this simple and
obvious truth and change our behavior, the sooner we
can get beyond our "self" and get on with fulfilling our
God-given purposes.

Contrary to the Ptolemy within us, the world does not revolve around us. Our comfort is not God's priority. If it is, something's gone awry. If we are the marquee event, how do we explain flat-earth challenges like death, disease, slumping economies, or rumbling earthquakes? If God exists to please us, then shouldn't we always be pleased?

Could a Copernican shift be in order? Perhaps our place is not at the center of the universe. God does not exist to make a big deal out of us. We exist to make a big deal out of him. It's not about you. It's not about me. It's about him. . . .

Such a shift comes so stubbornly, however. We've been demanding our way and stamping our feet since infancy. Aren't we all born with a default drive set on selfishness? "I want a spouse who makes me happy and coworkers who always ask my opinion. I want weather that suits me and traffic that helps me and a government that serves me. It's all about me."

Lucado spears us with a funny wake-up call—the one you didn't get from the soccer coach who wouldn't keep score because she insisted, "We're *all* winners, despite the other team scoring more goals!" You also didn't get it from your dad if he told you not to worry about passing the ball to the open guy on your periphery because "You're the best basketball player on the block . . . er, in the whole country! You're the next Michael Jordan, despite the fact you're a short white guy who can't jump!" And then you grew up and worked for a union boss who rejected merit pay proposals because "We're *all* equal so we all deserve to be compensated equally, despite varying degrees of productivity!"

Self-promotion. Self-preservation. Self-centeredness. It's all about me!

They all told us it was, didn't they? Weren't we urged to look out for number one? Find our place in the sun? Make a name for ourselves? We thought self-celebration would make us happy. . . .

But what chaos this philosophy creates. What if a symphony orchestra followed such an approach? Can you imagine an orchestra with an "It's all about me" outlook? Each artist clamoring for self-expression. Tubas blasting nonstop. Percussionists pounding to get attention. The cellist shoving the flutist out of the center-stage chair. The trumpeter standing atop the conductor's stool tooting his horn. Sheet music disregarded. Conductor ignored. What do you have but an endless tune-up session! . . .

No wonder our homes are so noisy, businesses so stress-filled, government so cutthroat, and harmony so rare. If you think it's all about you, and I think it's all about me, we have no hope for a melody. We've chased so many skinny rabbits that we've missed the fat one: the God-centered life.

What would happen if we took our places and played our parts? If we played the music the Maestro gave us to play? If we made his song our highest priority?

Would we see a change in families? We'd certainly HEAR a change. Less "Here is what I want!" More "What do you suppose God wants?"

What if a businessman took that approach? Goals of money and name making, he'd shelve. God-reflecting would dominate.

And your body? Ptolemaic thinking says, "It's mine; I'm going to enjoy it." God-centered thinking acknowledges, "It's God's; I have to respect it."

We'd see our suffering differently. "My pain proves God's absence" would be replaced with "My pain expands God's purpose."

Talk about a Copernican shift. Talk about a healthy shift. Life makes sense when we accept our place. The gift of pleasures, the purpose of problems—all for Him. The God-centered life works. And it rescues us from a life that doesn't.

But how do we make this kind of shift? How can we be bumped off self-center? Our ever-changing universe is to blame for making us think that we have to try to hold on to our perceived place of comfort—the center of it all. But finally opening our eyes to the revolving and evolving globe, the shifting sands and crashing waves, can also wake us up to the fact that change is an inevitable part of life.

That fact drives us toward some other kind of comfort. We must have a GPS set point, a guidepost. In my inaugural address as governor of Alaska, I spoke of setting my bearings by that Great North Star, which is depicted on our state flag. I told my fellow Alaskans that we were more fortunate than others, because we lived in a place that made it easy to stay on course. For we had the Great North Star with its steady light as our beacon bright, overhead in Alaska's expansive skies!

It turns out that Trig, barely two years old, has his own version of the Great North Star. When he was a tiny little bundle, maybe three months old, we noticed that he would often lie on his back and raise his right arm, staring at his hand for long periods of time. As he grew, the hand-staring continued with amazing consistency. When other objects were introduced to distract him, he'd look, he'd gurgle and giggle and stare for a bit, then turn back to his upraised hand.

I now notice that when my little guy is in unfamiliar settings, or perhaps is tired or feeling out of sorts, he pauses to look again at his hand. We joke when we see this, "Yep, Trig! The hand's still there! All is well." I've asked other mothers of children with Down syndrome if their child does the same. Often I hear that they do, and the theory is that staring at their hands is their baseline of comfort. It's a zone they get in to reassure themselves, to readjust internally in order to deal with some external discomfort.

Trig only recently became bold enough to want to step on beautiful, green grass. While visiting my relatives in Richland, Washington, Trig longed to play with Aunt Katie's sweet dogs amid their water bowls on the lawn behind the house. He had never before wanted to walk on anything but the sturdy flooring inside a house or on the pavement outside. But something had now changed and he couldn't resist.

Still not able to utter a word, Trig communicated how he would overcome his fear and reach his goal, the puppies. He would right himself as he gathered his courage by focusing on his Great North Star. He'd stare at his right hand. Take a step. Pause. Stare. Step. Cling to that beacon bright! Strength and comfort and security. *The hands! I can do this! This is better than walking on water! I've set my bearings and now I'm gonna pet that dog!* And he did!

We all navigate better with a North Star we can count on. Lucado lists promises in the Old and New Testaments that refer to our Creator's permanence. Romans 1:20 claims God's everlasting power. Daniel 6:26 and Psalm 59:16 show us where to go when we need a fortress and a refuge. It's there we can readjust, gather strength, take that step forward . . . stare at the hand . . . stare at the hand . . . walk toward the water bowl! All in the midst of inevitable change.

You want to hear about change? I've had more than my share in the last year and a half, thank you very much. It's as if God said to me, *Here, Sarah Palin, I've got a few things to add to your plate. You'd better have your compass pointed due north. May I suggest you get to know the intricacies of the vein pattern on the back of your right hand? You may want to stare at it once in awhile while I load this up.*

Thank God His outstretched hand was there through it all. Better His than my own. And thank God for America, whose exceptional culture smoothed the way for me, put out its arms to me, occasionally argued with me, but always welcomed me. My incredible experience over the past couple of years has made me more determined than ever that we can't lose this magic—we can't let go of the amazing mixture of tradition and innovation, of "clinging" to our own beliefs while we accommodate the beliefs of others—that has truly made this country great. Washington, Jefferson, Madison, and others built it. Tocqueville saw it. We live it. There is providence to this country. We can't lose sight of that.

It's been an exciting, productive, worthwhile period of tumult and change. Every chapter has been a teaching chapter and an opportunity to have affirmed what I always believed—that *everyone is battling something, everyone has a challenge.* But now I can more fully understand. There's no better place to experience it than in America. Thanks, Plato.

Conclusion

COMMONSENSE
CONSTITUTIONAL
CONSERVATISM

As I was finishing this book, Ted Stevens, America's longest-serving Republican senator, died in a plane crash in his beloved state of Alaska. Ted was always a warrior. He had survived combat flight missions in World War II. He was one of two survivors of a 1978 plane crash in Anchorage that killed his first wife, Ann. He battled prostate cancer and won. But by the time he died at age eighty-six, he had done much more than simply fight. He had succeeded. He had built a career serving the people of Alaska. In the process, he was instrumental in helping build the forty-ninth state—from the day he began, when we were only a territory, to the day he died, some fifty-one years after we joined the Union.

Sitting in a pew at his memorial service, I remembered a day from two years earlier, a sunny Saturday afternoon when I shared lunch with Ted at my kitchen table in Wasilla and discussed with him our mutual passion for developing Alaska's natural resources. Sometimes Ted and I had healthy disagreements over political angles, but more often he encouraged me in my public life. That day, he brought me a U.S. Senate coaster, which he had signed and inscribed with the encouraging words "Keep up what you are doing!" I knew then, as I know today, that his heart was always with the people of the last frontier. Ted Stevens spent his life in a worthy cause and inspired others to do the same.

Ted's death got me thinking about how much both Alaska and the country at large have changed since he began his distinguished political career. Alaska has come a long way from the virtual American colony it used to be—railing against a distant and all-encompassing federal government. Alaskans are slowly coming to enjoy the rights and shoulder the responsibilities of full citizenship. We have gained a (still-inadequate) measure of control over our destiny while coming to understand that, over the long term, addictions to Big Oil and Big Government are not in the best interests of our state.

America has changed, too, but in doing so we seem to have come full circle. In 1968, when Ted first became Alaska's senator, America was beset by economic problems at home and by a mortal enemy abroad, the Soviet Union. After a mediocre Carter presidency, which was characterized by a creeping national "malaise," in the 1980s we had a wondrous period of renewal under Ronald Reagan's visionary leadership. Thanks to the president's unfailing belief in our country, our economy recovered and "morning in America" replaced the seeming stagnancy of the preceding years. And because we were once again strong at home, we were also strong abroad. The cold war ended—and Reagan won—without a shot being fired.

Yet here we are, more than forty years later, back where we started, with a crisis of confidence at home and of security abroad. There's plenty of blame to go around for how we got here. Americans know in their hearts that both political parties are at fault. Both parties contributed to the overspending and government growth that is robbing our children of their future. Worst of all, both parties are part of the Washington culture of entitlement. This is the corrupt mind-set that has members of Congress writing tax laws for the rest of us, but failing to pay their own taxes, and crooked legislators being caught with their fingers in the till, refusing to live by the same laws and standards as the people who pay their salaries. No wonder millions of Americans are up in arms (figuratively, of course), demanding relief from the "change" Barack Obama and the left have thrust upon them against their will.

When President Obama was elected in 2008, some members of the media resurrected the Reagan theme and called it "morning in America" again. Obama was compared to FDR and JFK. And as hard as I campaigned for him *not* to be president, I shared the feeling of almost desperate hope that many other Americans felt. Like them—like you—I love my country and I want it to succeed. But a new morning in America hasn't broken over the Capitol dome. We're not succeeding in Washington. America is losing her way there; losing the sense of herself as an exceptional nation.

The reason, I think, is that we have leaders today in Washington who don't share this fundamental view of American greatness. I thought of this disconnect recently when I was watching the Blue Angels at the Alaska Air Show at Elmendorf Air Force Base. There I was, brought to tears by the magnificence of these amazing aviators, when my brother, knowing what I was thinking, handed me a note. Scribbled in black Sharpie on the back of his entrance ticket was the message "I'd rather have an army of sheep led by a lion than an army of lions led by a sheep."

Various forms of this quote have been attributed to everyone from Alexander the Great to Napoleon, but I knew what my brother meant. There we were, looking at these great lions of the sky, overwhelmed by love of country and appreciation for America's finest: our men and women in uniform. But who was leading them? And to what end?

We have a president, perhaps for the first time since the founding of our republic, who expresses his belief that America is not the greatest earthly force for good the world has ever known. Now, I know that sounds a little overblown to many educated liberals, a little jingoistic. But so many of us *do* believe America is that exceptional force for good. America is not a perfect place. We have made mistakes, and allowed some terrible things in our history. Given the sordid historical record of virtually every other country on this planet,

however, I think our pride in America is perfectly justified. Yet our current president seems to see nothing
uniquely admirable in the American experience. Nothing uniquely admirable about an America that fought
two world wars and sought not one inch of territory
or one dollar of plunder. Nothing uniquely admirable
about an America that laid the foundation for freedom
and security in Europe and Asia after World War II.
And nothing uniquely admirable about an America
that prevailed in the cold war not by military might
but, above all, by the truth of our ideas against an evil,
inhuman ideology.

The consequences of this average-to-below-average
view of our country are profound, both at home and
abroad. Indeed, especially abroad. A prominent Czech
official has called America's current foreign policy
"enemy-centric," and I think he's on to something. An
enemy-centric foreign policy is one that seems more interested in coddling adversaries (in Washington, they
call this "outreach" or "resetting relations") and apologizing than in standing up to enemies and sticking by
principles—among which are friendship and support
for our fellow democracies. The current foreign policy
is one that values the opinion of European elites more
than the freedom of Iranian democrats. It's a view of
the world in which an Arizona law enforcing federal

immigration policy is equated with forced abortions in China. It's leadership that can crow about fulfilling its promise to withdraw our troops from Iraq without once uttering the word *victory*.

At home, this president's rejection of American exceptionalism has translated into a stark lack of faith in the American people. There's no other way to describe a governing philosophy that won't trust individual Americans to control their own health care, plan for their own retirement, or even spend their own money. What our current leaders don't seem to understand is that American greatness—and success abroad—begins at home. It begins with faith and trust in the fundamental goodness, creativity, entrepreneurialism, and generosity of the American people. America is incapable of going abroad in pursuit of anything less than its principles. Yes, we make mistakes, and, no, we are not, nor do we wish to be, the world's sole policeman, banker, or nanny. But the fact is that we have been a force for good in the world. To deny this, or to seek to ignore or downplay it, is to deny the sacrifice of the thousands upon thousands of patriotic men and women who brought about this good.

Ronald Reagan is remembered for many qualities: his communication skills, his principles, his optimism. But perhaps the single greatest reason we love and admire Reagan is because he loved and admired us. He had boundless faith in the American people because he had boundless faith in the American idea. We are endowed by our Creator with freedom. And we have managed to be, for the most part, the moral and upright people capable of living in freedom that our Founders hoped we would be. We have preserved and expanded our own freedom while extending that gift to other peoples around the world. Reagan paid us the tribute of respecting these undeniable truths, not as some kind of political pose or out of narrow-minded patriotism, but because he understood that it was best for us and, ultimately, for the world to honor what makes us exceptional. Reagan understood what President Obama doesn't—or at least won't admit: young Afghan women struggling to go to school in Kabul and students fighting for democracy in Tehran don't want America to be an ordinary nation any more than we do.

Whenever I give a speech—whenever I'm in a room with more than a few people in it, for that matter—I like to ask everyone to take the time to thank a vet. It is easily one of the most sincere sentiments we can express. The reason, of course, is that Americans are truly, profoundly grateful to our military men and women—not because they have sacrificed for land or power or oil, but because they have fought for, protected, and defended *freedom*. Our God-given liberty is the exceptional principle at the heart of this exceptional nation. That's why we are different. It is why we have become a nation composed of all the peoples of the earth, all assimilated in this beautiful melting pot. It is also why we have a special role to play in the world. And if we don't honor our freedom at home, we can't expect to see it honored and preserved anywhere else.

We are still, as Reagan said, "the abiding alternative to tyranny." We are still the shining city on a hill, a beacon for all who seek freedom and prosperity. I'm thankful President Obama understands that our security does depend in part on reaching out in friendship to other nations. But the nation that extends its hand in reconciliation and peace has to know what it believes—and be ready and able to back it up; otherwise that extended hand is just a foolish gesture. It is not in America's interest—or the interest of the peace-loving nations of the world—to project weakness to terrorists and tyrants.

The world will not be more peaceful if America doesn't believe in herself and her greatness. It will, instead, become more dangerous and violent. Without this belief, it would be saying to Americans, *You're no city on a hill. You have nothing to offer the world. You're what we say you are—nothing more, nothing less.*

I don't believe this. More important, I don't believe my fellow Americans do, either.

The question, going forward, is how? How do we embrace our exceptionalism at home and abroad? How do we take this great awakening among the American people and turn it into a positive force for reclaiming our country and our heritage? Like so many Americans, I have been thinking about this a lot lately.

The answer is closer than many of us realize. We don't need a manifesto. We don't need a new party. We just need to honor what our country is and was meant to be. And we need to remember the common sense most of us learned before we went to kindergarten.

If I have to label myself, I would happily slap on a sticker that read "Commonsense Constitutional Conservative." I am an Alaskan, with the inbred spirit of independence we are so proud of in our state, and I am proud to have been registered in the Republican Party since I was eighteen, because I believe that the planks of our platform are the strongest foundation upon which to build a great nation while protecting our God-given liberties.

Some say we don't actually have a two-party system, that each party is the party of big government, with a Republican wing that likes wars, deficits, and assaults on civil liberties, and a Democrat wing that likes welfare, taxes, and assaults on commercial laissez-faire. There's some truth to this idea. While Republicans and Democrats certainly differ on many issues, sometimes the outcome is the same, because in some respects both parties think they know what is best, and will use the coercive power of the state to impose and enforce their agendas.

If Democrats are driving the country toward socialism at a hundred miles per hour, while the Republicans are driving at only fifty, commonsense constitutional conservatives want to turn the car around. We want to get back to the basics that have made this country great—the fundamental values of family, faith, and flag that I have talked about in this book.

The mainstream media and some on the left gleefully tell us there are lunatics and racists in the Tea Party movement who are taking over the right-wing asylum. I think we all understand what motivates this kind of divisive talk. The fact is that Americans of all political persuasions are awakening to two firm sources of unity: our founding Charters of Liberty, and the virtues necessary to live up to them.

Maintaining a healthy republic requires a populace that adheres to those old-fashioned values of hard work, honesty, integrity, thrift, and courage. It is entirely right for us as a society to discuss the best way to foster those values. And after a half century of liberal social experimentation, we know what does this. It's family (when we talk about limited local government, it means the state knows better than the feds, the city knows better than the state, and the family knows better than the city). It's faith (be it through religion or the moral values transmitted in our secular culture). And it's flag (the understanding that we are an exceptional nation with an exceptional message for the world).

This is the firm, hallowed ground on which we all can stand. For me, the idea of unity among common-sense Americans, regardless of their voter registration, is not a difficult concept to grasp. Most of my friends and family members are and always have been inde-pendent. Combine my social and familial surroundings with the Alaskan spirit of self-reliance with which I was raised, and commonsense unity sort of comes naturally.

It would be wise for us to use the common founda-tions of our republic and the virtues that sustain it to find a new way forward. Commonsense constitutional conservatism is about rediscovering our founding ideals and striving to be a nation that does justice to them.

As I look forward to the future, I know that my chil-dren, and their children, will live in a state and a coun-try that are in many ways different from the ones in which I grew up. We won't necessarily share the same experiences. But I hope and pray that we share the same bedrock beliefs.

It is our responsibility to preserve and pass on those beliefs. For there *are* beliefs that define us as Americans. They are the source of our prosperity, our tolerance, our spirit of innovation, and our greatness. They are carved into our foundation stone. They have been defended by the blood of patriots. We can and should debate what they mean and how they are best preserved. We can and should call each other out when we fall short of our beliefs. We can and should always strive to live up to them. But they are still there, eternally defining and guiding the greatest country in the history of the world. And they are what make the citizens of this great country Americans—not by blood, or race, or creed, but by heart. May we always be so.

ACKNOWLEDGMENTS

As always, I thank my family, my inspiration. Thank you for circling the wagons and providing generous support. I love you. May God keep shining on you all!

To those who are true friends—you know who you are because you're still here—plus our good helpers for the kids and tasks at hand, we can't do anything without you. Thank you!

I could not have written this book were it not for our veterans, our past and present patriots in uniform who are our true heroes. Your protection of our freedom to embrace faith and family under the flag allows America to be exceptional.

Huge appreciation goes to those who tell the truth in the media arena. Those willing to seek and report truth encourage us to keep our heads up and forge ahead. You Commonsense Constitutionalists who take the shots every day (and have been doing it a lot longer than I have) yet you never retreat—keep it up. Freedom depends on you. The same goes for Prayer Warriors lifting up our country. Keep the faith.

I want to thank attorney Robert Barnett and the HarperCollins team for invaluable assistance with this book, with a special thanks to the brilliant, independent self-starter who got her start in Alaska, Jessica Gavora. Thank you for your most important work on *America by Heart*. We started out on opposing teams on the high school parquet, but our Alaskan roots connected us and shall grow into the influence we believe America can use today. You are an amazing Mama Grizzly.

Grateful acknowledgment is made for permission to reprint from the following:

Bill Banuchi, excerpt from "Healthcare for America: A Biblical and Moral Imperative" from http://billbanuchi.blogspot.com/2009/08/healthcare-for-america-biblical-and.html. Used by permission of Rev. Bill Banuchi, Marriage and Family Savers Institute.

Michael Bowker, excerpt from "The Loudest Cheer" from *Reader's Digest* (May 1994). Copyright © 1994 by Reader's Digest Association, Inc. Reprinted with the permission of Reader's Digest.

Colleen Carroll Campbell, excerpt from "Pro-Life Feminism Is the Future" from *The Washington Post* (May 23, 2010). Copyright © 2010 by Colleen Carroll Campbell. Reprinted with the permission of the author, www.colleen-campbell.com.

Mary Kate Cary, excerpt from "The New Conservative Feminist Movement" from *U.S. News & World Report* (June 23, 2010). Copyright © 2010 by U.S. News & World Report. Reprinted with permission.

THE NEW LUXURY IN READING

We hope you enjoyed reading
our new, comfortable print size and found it
an experience you would like to repeat.

Well – you're in luck!

HarperLuxe offers the finest in fiction and
nonfiction books in this same larger print size and
paperback format. Light and easy to read, HarperLuxe
paperbacks are for book lovers who want to see
what they are reading without the strain.

For a full listing of titles and
new releases to come, please visit our website:

www.HarperLuxe.com